SINGLE AND

SATISFIED

SINGLE AND
SATISFIED

AUDREY LEE SANDS

TYNDALE HOUSE PUBLISHERS
Wheaton, Illinois

Cloverdale House Publishers Ltd., London, England

Library of Congress Catalog Card Number
70-123295 ISBN 8423-5890-0

Copyright © 1971 by Tyndale House Publishers, Wheaton, Illinois 60187. All rights
reserved.

Fifth printing, October 1973
Printed in the United States of America

CONTENTS

1

SELECTED FOR SERVICE

Not a fragment of sound penetrated the darkness of Elaine's room. It was as if the world itself had taken off its shoes and was standing still, breathless before God.

Elaine lay, hands under her head, staring up at nothing. But the darkness was illuminated by the inner glow in her heart. The total blackness around her, blotting out the walls and the furniture, seemed only to add to the sense of being in the presence of God.

The missionary convention was over. She had sat through many of them before (her church had one every year) but this year had been different. Each night the message had been an arrow to her heart, as were the pictures showing the dark faces of heathendom. There was a look of utter hopelessness on some, and from the eyes of others flamed the very essence of Satanic power. It made her shudder.

Was there no one to liberate them from themselves and the powers of darkness? Why, why did there seem to be so few to tell them — tell them who could free them? O God, send more people to tell them!

Me?

Not me! How could I? Anyway, Lord, I'm only eighteen. There would be so much training ahead. They need help now. And — and, Lord, there's Rick. You know he wants to be an engineer. Oh, no — no. No!

For a week she had grappled with herself against that strange conviction that God was calling her. Her heart felt as if it would break with the pressure. Then tonight the choir had sung:

> "Where he leads me I will follow;
> Where he leads me I will follow.
> I'll go with him, with him all the way."

Suddenly she had sprung from her seat beside Rick. Throwing herself on her knees at the front pew, the pent-up emotion within her broke.

Now it was all over. She was home in bed with the lights out.

Peace — relief — yes, they were there. But the thought of Rick brought a brief stinging to her eyes. The ride home in the car after the service had been silent. She knew that he did not understand, but the experience had been too sacred to try to explain to him at the moment. Surely her

Heavenly Father who was calling her would work that out too.

School. Training. When? Where? There were so many questions. The future lay so vast before her. And why? Was this all an emotional reaction? What made her think that God was calling *her* to be a missionary? Surely this conviction hadn't all been whipped up in one concentrated week of appeal?

Was it the suggestion, after she had spoken at the district young people's rally a couple of months ago, that she ought to use her talent for speaking on the mission field? She had some musical talents too — the lessons she had taken on her guitar should be used somehow. People always told her she played it very well.

Now that she thought about it, maybe it was the two months of social studies in her senior year in high school that had gotten to her. They had studied some of the South Pacific islands. The people looked so interesting; the jungles, so intriguing — and just think, in some of these places the gospel had never been preached.

There was another thing too. She had become so disgusted with the lack of interest in her church young people's group. There seemed to be so little concern for the spiritual needs of others. Could she ever forget the night last June when she had been speaking particularly eloquently (she thought) about the spiritual darkness of a certain island tribe, and Tony had scathingly cut her short with: "Oh, can it. So what! You sound like you thought the world would fall apart just because a few heathen are going to hell. Missions are okay, but you don't need to get carried away!" It still made Elaine burn to think about it.

Then, too, things hadn't been going too smoothly with Rick lately. But, she told herself, it would pass. Every romance had to be a little stormy, didn't it? Nevertheless, they did seem to be growing apart. She tucked that thought back into the mental box out of which it had come and snapped down the lid.

All these thoughts were pushed aside by another. Hadn't she been asking God daily for the last two years to show her his perfect will for her life? After all, that had to be at the bottom of any right choice. The trouble was, she hadn't really expected things to go this way.

Sleep began to claim her consciousness. As it did, the feeling crept over her that the test of her daily giving of her life over to God for these last two years had come. "Lord, if this is what you have for me, I want it. But you will have to work it out for me. It all seems so big and even confusing. Yet, 'I know whom I have believed and am persuaded that he is able to keep that. . . .' "

A unique happening? No. In the intense glow of a stirring appeal, hundreds, even thousands, of young people like Elaine have dedicated their lives to serving Christ on foreign soil.

It may have happened to you. If some experience in your life led you to make this kind of commitment, then what? Have you, like Elaine, stopped to wonder just what brought you to that moment of decision when you decided to be a missionary? If you haven't thought about it, you should.

What motivated you? What got you so excited about that little village and those people? What made you so concerned about those students, that little island, those Tibetan refugees?

What aroused you?

What made you think you were needed there? Why do you want to go?

Before you pack your barrels, you need to ask the Lord to help you clearly evaluate your motives. Why do you believe God is calling you? Sometimes tragic mistakes have been made. The motives seemed, at the time, to be the best; but they were wrong. They didn't come from the true source of missionary motivation. And then, at best, the Lord has had to spend much precious time straightening out a missionary's goals and ambitions. He has had to spend long years in getting enough of the missionary out of the way so that he, Christ, could be glorified through their lives and labors.

Now, dig out *your* box of commitment and pry off the lid. Take a good look at what you find inside. Some of the contents may surprise you. It's possible that some of the motives you find carefully packed away in there are motives you never realized you had. Maybe you were aware of some but never guessed that they could be wrong. Do you have some wrong motives in your box of commitment?

Take talents, for example. This is a rather delicate subject. Someone tells you your talent would be of great value on a particular field or in some specialized missionary ministry. Presto, you are confronted with pride. Is your concern only that your talent be used, or do you want his perfect will in your life? Do you want to glorify him at any cost, under any circumstances — whether he chooses to use your talent or not? Dig clear to the bottom of your commitment box for that one. You may discover that your "call" was an attempt on your part to make people notice your ability.

Another question. Why are you thinking of that certain field and people? Excitement, perhaps? Glamor? Has your interest been aroused because the place or the people sound fascinating and appeal to your imagination?

A missionary call became a driving force in my life when at the age of thirteen, I heard a missionary speak about Borneo, or West Kalimantan, as it is now called. For years I hung onto the place as well as the call. Even when I was in Bible school I would envision myself in the jungles of Borneo: I was shooting rapids in a dugout canoe to get to the villages; I was stepping over snakes and killing scorpions; shoe leather was rotting in the humid, sticky climate; I was teaching unclad savages and reaping a great harvest of souls.

The personal appeal and glamor of the jungle was the biggest attraction. But the call itself *was* real; I was just facing in the wrong direction. And it took the Lord two or three years, along with some difficult and strange experiences, to turn me toward the field of *his* choice, one which had almost no personal appeal.

Who wanted to do technical missionary work in the middle of a big, civilized city? Not the girl who didn't like cities. Not the girl who loved the mountains and the wilds. Not the girl with the pioneer spirit. Not the girl who imagined herself shooting rapids, fighting snakes, climbing jungle trails, and winning dozens of naked savages for the Lord.

No, it wasn't the direction I had dreamed of. But the Lord knew what he was doing. Had I followed my dreams and chosen what was personally appealing, I would have missed the most interesting and satisfying place of ministry. The Lord had a place for me, and he evidently had fitted me for it.

What about you? God will give you a love for the place and the people to which he sends you. Don't worry about that. Be most concerned about God's perfect will in the matter. Leave the details to him. He can handle every one of them perfectly. You'll discover God knows more about what is personally appealing to you than you do. After all, he created you!

Now, dig around in that commitment box a little more.

Are your missionary motives colored — at least along the edges — with a lonely heart, dissatisfaction with life, or boredom? Have you thought, "I'll go to the mission field where the missionaries and the natives need me and will appreciate me"? It's a subtle idea, and dangerous. If you are not allowing the Lord to fill your heart with his love and sufficiency at home, how do you expect to overflow with his love on the field? Your problems will only be greatly multiplied there.

Sometimes single girls are the brunt of joking remarks to the effect that we are going to the field because it's the best place to bury a broken heart after a romance that didn't work out. Well, is it true? Am I the only one who has run into single missionaries who can't fill an evening of conversation with much more than stories of the "fish that got away"?

No, just because a girl talks a lot about her love affairs it doesn't necessarily mean that she turned to missionary life out of frustration and loneliness. Sometimes one can't help but wonder, though!

Back to the commitment box. There is another missionary motive that looks bright and shiny on the surface. You've at least heard of it; well-meaning promoters of evangelical missions use it quite frequently. It sounds good, but bears a close examination. You are told, "The need is the call." Does this constitute a good motive? Well, yes and no. Certainly the need is the reason God calls you. Human need is the basis for all missionary endeavor. But you are going to be a missionary because that is God's will for *your* life. If the need were the only call, then every Christian who stayed home would be disobedient. And that certainly cannot be right.

How often have you been led to think, after hearing a missionary speaker, that the heathen not only need you, they want you and are waiting with open arms for you? That would be nice if it were true in more than a very few cases, but people blinded by the powers of darkness don't *want* light.

"Every wrongdoer hates the light and will not come out into the light, but shrinks from it, lest his works, his deeds, his activities, and his conduct, be exposed and reproved." That's the way John 3:20 is presented in the Amplified Bible. General indifference or outright hostility to you and your message is what you will usually find. Satan sees to that. After all, it's his territory you are invading.

More than one missionary has been confused and bitterly disappointed to find no one wanted him. The need is there, all right. But knowing there is a need will never take you through the difficult times of testing that are bound to come. You must be convinced of God's specific call in *your* life. You must know that God called you to the particular place to which you are going.

How can one know God's call? If you're a sincere Christian young person, you've looked for the answer to that question many times.

It seems complicated, but is it? Perhaps it just appears complex because there is no pat answer, no answer on the stock shelf to fit every occasion. There's a good reason for that: the answer is as unique and individual as the person who asks the question.

If God is specifically calling you, see if God is revealing to you his specific plan for your life, then the answer *has* to be as individual and personal as you are. That is the wonderful part about our relationship to Christ. It has no duplicates, no mimeographed copies. It is unique and personal, because we are.

No mail-order catalogue can list a stock set of answers to the question of what God's will is for your life. But there are answers — personal, individual, and unique. And there are ways to find those answers.

Here are a few guidelines to direct your search.

You do have to consider the need. Expose yourself to it. Learn all you can about the needs of many fields. Learn about the people. Find out what types of missionary service are needed. Explore the technical needs as well. Writers and editors are needed where illiteracy is being eliminated. There's missionary radio to consider, teaching, nursing, secretarial work, linguistics — the list is almost endless.

Take into consideration your own circumstances, your training, your abilities, and your interests.

Most important of all, ask God for the personal conviction of the Holy Spirit as to your place and type of ministry. Ask him with a broken and open heart. Don't be afraid to ask God for his perfect will at any cost, for "Even the Son of Man learned obedience by the things that he suffered." No price is too great to pay for God's best, even if it means letting go of some of your most cherished dreams. No life has greater rewards than one given completely to him.

Sometimes finding the Lord's will is complicated because we fail to walk close to him.

On deputation I was sharing a room with the daughter of the family with whom I was staying. She was a Christian — a college girl about my own age. But in many ways I could see that she was a self-centered rebel.

One morning I woke up and, naturally, I started

talking casually about where I was going and why. Suddenly the girl sat up in bed and asked in a fiercely defiant tone, "And just how do you know that what you are doing is the Lord's will for your life?"

The question stung. Would you have an answer? Could you explain your own assurance?

Did you ever run across a bride of four or five months who had to ask her husband if he took sugar in his coffee? Of course not! She undoubtedly knew that before they were married. Imagine that after five years of married life a wife should say to her husband, "I was going to buy you a new tie today, but I didn't know what type you would like." Ridiculous!

The husband-and-wife relationship is an intimate one. The wife who does not know that her husband prefers conservative ties probably is not sensitive to any of his feelings and is certainly not very observant. It probably follows that their marriage relationship is neither close nor happy.

Is it any more ridiculous to say that you don't have the faintest idea how the Lord may be leading you in the big steps of life if you have a close day-by-day walk with him? Will you be in the dark and feel your Heavenly Father is a stranger if you read his word every day and experience close communion through prayer? Is God a blank wall to those who make a daily commitment of every detail of their lives? If you strive daily to please him in every minor area of your life, will there be a problem when the big things come up?

The closer you walk with the Lord, the more

sensitive to him you will be. The Holy Spirit's guidance will always be obvious for at least one step
at a time. That's all you really need, isn't it? Naturally there may be a few difficult or even confusing
times; but if your heart's desire is to know his will
in every area of your life, you will be able to con-
fidently step out as he points the way and makes
it possible for you to do his will.

One of the most wonderful Scripture passages for
guidance that I know of is Isaiah 30:20, 21 (RSV).
"And though the Lord give you the bread of adversity and the water of affliction, yet your Teacher
will not hide himself any more, but your eyes shall
see your Teacher. And your ears shall hear a word
behind you, saying, 'This is the way, walk in it,'
when you turn to the right or when you turn to the
left." Listen for his voice. He will guide you if you
have a sensitive relationship to him.

One missionary said that when she was a girl of
ten, a wise Sunday school superintendent started a
Bible-reading contest. From that she developed the
habit of a daily quiet time which she never dropped.
This habit led her into a sensitive relationship with
her Lord.

Many things and many people came into her life,
as they do in all lives. They could have led her a
hundred different directions. When the call to missionary service came, it was very unexpected. The
decision must have seemed to some to be made on
the spur of the moment. She said, "When it came,
such peace and assurance from the Lord came with
it, I couldn't even pray about it. I just knew it was
what the Lord wanted me to do and could only

thank him for it. I have never once doubted that call, despite the deep valleys he has sometimes led me through in my missionary experience. What a comfort to be able to say, 'Lord, I don't know what you're doing, or how, but I know it is you who has led me thus far. I'll trust you the rest of the way.' "

No two missionaries have exactly the same experience. But one thing is certain. You can't treat God like an accessory to be used at your convenience and then one day rush into his presence with, "So what do you want me to do, now that I'm out of school and facing life?"

The basic principles of the spiritual life are the same for everyone. If you walk close to him, you can trust him to lead you and give you perfect assurance of his will in your life. And that assurance will be the sure foundation that will carry you through the often difficult circumstances of missionary life.

How about that commitment box? Does it need a little spring cleaning, or perhaps even some fumigating? Have you found your call to missionary service cluttered with dubious motives? Is there a desire for self-satisfaction, personal happiness, and fulfillment?

Ask God to strip you of all but that basic desire to have his perfect will — to glorify him only, no matter what the cost to self. Begin a closer daily walk with the Lord. Consult him about the decisions of every area of your life. Seek his pleasure concerning all your activities. Learn to walk in his way constantly. If you do that, you will have assurance about the big steps in your life. You will know the assurance of Abraham's servant who said, "I being in the way, the Lord led me."

Then when the rains come down and the floods of adversity come up, you will not be left floundering in doubt about your calling. Rather experience will serve to further conform you to his image and bring you to an even higher plane of satisfying assurance and contentment in himself.

2

SELECTED TO BE SINGLE

"Dress up? Why? There's no one interesting or eligible within a hundred miles. When it comes to men, around here we've had a crop failure."

"A new quarterback, huh! Good looking and unattached? This I've got to see."

"Dad! Answer the door, please! I'll die — I'll simply die if Paul sees me in this dress!"

"I never wear green. My boss says it's unbecoming to me."

"He's Betty's boyfriend? Hmm. Well, that can be changed."

Sound familiar? The heart of every true woman centers around her relationship to men, and rightfully so. It's the way God created us.

Have you faced the fact? Have you faced yourself as a woman? Or have you pushed your womanly thoughts aside and not laid them honestly before the Lord. Why? Could it be because they give you a bit of a guilty feeling? After all, you say, isn't a spiritually depraved world more important than your womanly desires? Perhaps your refusal to examine these desires is heightened by the lack of romance in the foreseeable future. You have forced beneath the surface the secret longings of your heart and set a determined face to the field without allowing yourself to be confronted with the reality of your own human nature.

If that is what you have done — stop now! You're human. You need companionship. God knows you need companionship. (You've told him often enough, haven't you?) And yet you're still single, and you're on your way to the field. Does that mean God has overlooked you? Does that mean that he expects you to make a special superhuman sacrifice? Perhaps, but don't get a martyr complex.

The fact that you are a woman who needs companionship doesn't prevent God from calling you to the field single. It's happened before, many times. He calls you, knowing you are a woman. He knows your heart better than you do, and he wants you to bare that heart honestly before him. He knows that it is the most difficult question a girl can ever ask herself, but still he wants you to face up to it: "Am I prepared to give up marriage — forever — if that is God's will?"

Earthshaking? It probably will be to any normal girl if she is honest with herself and with the Lord. After all, who doesn't want to share in the most holy and blessed of all human relationships?

Perhaps you're like one missionary girl who felt the call of God on her life for foreign missionary service in her early teens. It never entered her mind until nearly ten years later that the Lord would ask her to go single.

With your built-in desires for human love and companionship, how can you look into the future and say, "Lord, I don't know what you have in store for me, but I am prepared to live without a husband's love and companionship. I'm prepared to be content only in you, for a whole lifetime, if that is your will."

A lifetime! That's normally a long time. It takes you through the bright, vigorous teens and twenties when it is sheer delight to share all the excitement and adventures of youth with a man: a football game, a walk on a lake shore on a moonlit night, a hayride, or a hike, perhaps a search together into some field of study, the joy of watching a wee baby develop. Then there are the golden thirties and forties when life is full and rich, when you are mature and your desire is for home and family life. And when middle age comes, it carries with it the growing desire to sit back a bit and enjoy the fruits of your labors and your grandchildren. Then, who would deny that the declining years of life are the very hardest in which to be alone?

Can you in one moment sweep aside the cherished thoughts of a life companionship with an act of commitment to God? Can you really say, "Thy will be done"? It sounds like too much for God to ask. Humanly, a joyful and lasting commitment like that is impossible. Yet the question of marriage must be faced. It must explicitly be laid on the altar before you go to the field single. Whether or not you marry must be left entirely up to him. There must be no strings attached if you are to lead a completely useful and happy life on the field and not be a burden to other fellow missionaries who will have to add your lonely, discontented heart to their own problems.

How, then, are you to go about making a God-enabled commitment of that kind? Commitment to God depends not only on sentiment and emotion, but also on the will — a very definite act of the will. Perhaps you don't want to be satisfied with God alone. You want to find satisfaction in a flesh-and-blood man, not in a spiritual entity. You refuse to give this all important issue to him. In effect, you tell the Lord that you don't believe he can fill the need for companionship in your life that a man could fill. The spiritual aspect of a man or a woman cannot be separated from the physical; perhaps you have never learned personally that the physical can be lifted, satisfied, and filled by the spiritual. Jesus Christ is both God and man and is therefore the divine answer to every human need.

When you take God as the literal answer to all that you need in every area of your life, what then? Do you become so heavenly-minded, so pious, so obnoxiously "good" that you lose your humanness? Will no one care to associate with you because you have become so "unbelievably" spiritual? Certainly not! The closer a person walks with the Lord, the more delightful a person he or she is. You cherish his friendship and love being around him.

What real man or woman of God doesn't, in your opinion and estimation, have a very distinct and pleasing character? Many even have brilliant personalities. The Holy Spirit living in complete control of our lives does not distort or take away our personality. He lifts every peak of natural charm and individuality to its highest and best. At the same time he minimizes our faults. It's like throwing a golden robe over an old beat-up arm chair. The chair still retains its shape, but it looks like a throne.

Do not be afraid to give God everything — even your deepest longings and desires. He will set you at liberty from the frustrations of human desire. He will beautify your character and personality. He will make you a very much more wonderful person than you are. And you will be much better prepared for a happy marriage should he eventually bring that your way.

There is no better preparation for commitment to a husband than commitment to Christ. If you know what it means to obey your Lord out of love and devotion, it won't be difficult to be submissive to your husband. If you have become one with Christ in heart and mind, it won't be hard for you to identify with a life companion. If you have sought to understand and to delight in the will of your Heavenly Father, then you will have a minimum of marital adjustment problems. The more perfectly you love the Lord, the more perfect will be your marriage relationship. It was not by chance that the Holy Spirit chose the marriage relationship to symbolize Christ's relationship to the Church.

One of the most striking examples we have in Scripture of the total commitment of natural affections to the Lord is found in the willingness of Abraham to sacrifice his son Isaac. Abraham loved his only son, through whom all the promised seed of Abraham was to come. Abraham's fatherly heart must have been in agony when twelve-year-old Isaac asked on the way to Mount Moriah, "Dad, we have the wood and the fire, but where is the sacrifice?" Yet, lifting his desperate heart once more to his God and Heavenly Father, Abraham triumphed over natural affection, reason, and self-will, and in faith answered, "God will provide."

The process of learning to trust God each moment — for that is what total commitment to God is — can be difficult at times. God may have to sweep out from under you all human crutches and supports. God tested *my* commitment to him by actually taking from me what I had given to him — the masculine companionship I'd enjoyed all my life.

Though nearly ten years separated us, my two older brothers and I were always great pals. As a youngster I stood by chattering and pumping them with questions as they worked on old cars. I don't know how many times one brother explained to me the principle of combustion in a gasoline motor. They were already married when I was in high school, but both had pastorates in the vicinity, and we were able to spend a good bit of time together as real friends.

After high school I went to Bible school, and again there was constant opportunity for masculine fellowship. One friend even had an optimistic eye on the future. The relationship did not become permanent, however, as we both recognized that it was not God's will.

Almost a year to the day after graduation, I sailed to the field — single. I left in the midst of great joy and anticipation for all that the Lord had ahead. My heart was so full it nearly burst.

But I never knew what it would be like to be without masculine companionship until it was taken away from me. Then the shoe of commitment began to pinch.

By the end of my first year on the field, though still very happy in the work, I began to feel deep depression resulting from lack of companionship and friendship with the opposite sex. It was a feeling of inadequacy, a feeling that no man would ever really want me anyhow. But our Lord has a great understanding heart. Right at that time a fine young man paid a prolonged visit to a neighboring missionary family. Our paths quickly crossed. We were of kindred minds and enjoyed each other's fellowship to the full. He was a pleasure to be with, and he knew how to treat a woman like a queen without leading her on.

That short period of masculine companionship fully restored my lost confidence in my own femininity. The depression lifted. When he left, I missed him, and commitments had to be strengthened with the Lord; but I saw the wonderful hand of the Heavenly Father in allowing me that time. He had not been trying to downgrade me as a woman. He only wanted me to trust him more fully to meet those womanly needs.

Another year passed, and then came a jolt. I suddenly realized that what I craved was not marriage. The Lord had indeed helped me to lay that aside. There was something else. Except for brief exchanges of conversation over our work, I was completely cut off from masculine minds. Frantically I wondered if I would ever be able to communicate with a man again.

At the time I was the only single girl living with several families, all of them fairly young. All the men with whom I worked were married. That meant I was rightfully cut off from real fellowship with them. I shall never forget the day this realization hit me. I went to my apartment and cried for hours. Finally, on my knees, I said another big "yes" to the Lord. "All right, Lord, you've taken me this far. Now if you want me to be forever barred from a conversation with a man about anything except work and weather, all right. Take that too. I want you to be, and I know that you can be, all that I need in my life." Was that a ridiculously extreme commitment? When the Lord asks, he asks for all. When we have said "yes" to all, then he can in his wisdom and grace and love give back the portion he knows will not hurt us. And of course, that is exactly what he has done for me. There has been abundant opportunity for stimulating fellowship with fellow laborers and others.

From time to time the whole issue of masculine companionship has to be recommitted. Sometimes there comes a temptation to feel sorry for yourself. An overwhelming emotion sweeps over you as you look out on a breathtaking scene. There's a surge of desire to have a masculine hand in yours — someone with whom to share the beauty. How many fresh commitments I have made to God as I watched the moon make a golden path across the sea, a scene I could see often from my apartment.

Sometimes the whole issue arises all over again when you are presented with a physically difficult situation which under normal conditions a man would handle. Perhaps it is when you're alone in a dangerous spot at night with a flat tire. What a temptation it is to feel sorry for yourself while you are frantically changing it in the pitch dark, half expecting at any moment that somebody might grab you from behind. (I had my tire-changing time down to eleven minutes with one old car I used.)

It is times like these that the Lord can be the most precious. Do not sink into self-pity. The only way to handle such experiences is to lift your heart instantly in adoration and praise to your Lord. Tell him once more that you love him and that is all you need. The floods of joy and contentment, even to a very sore heart, can be overwhelming. There will come the sweet realization that he is your constant companion, friend, and protector. You really need no other.

If you wish, there's a method guaranteed to shatter your contentment in the Lord. Build air castles over a man you used to know or one you would like to know. Dream a little. Indulge in a few moments of self-pity. You'll be in trouble every time! (Take it from one who has allowed herself to fall into this pit many times.)

The enemy longs to take our minds off the Lord.

He knows that the Lord alone can supply the very thing we most desire. Committing all to the Lord means wanting him to be everything to you. Open your heart and allow him to be just that. That's what David said in Psalm 37:4: "Delight thyself also in the Lord; and he shall give thee the desires of thine heart." Delight yourself in his overflowing love and grace. Delight yourself in his understanding and wisdom. He will give you the desires of your heart; he will fill your longing heart with his love and companionship; he will satisfy you with his friendship; and you will experience the sheer beauty and perfectness of his love.

Do you believe it? Are you willing to know what it means to give God all, including your right to marriage, before you even go to the field? The commitment will be hard — the hardest you ever made — but its dividends will be priceless. If you don't make that commitment, the chances are very great that you will experience heartbreak and continual frustration. Not only will you suffer, but so will your missionary co-workers. Even the fruit of your ministry will be stunted by your constantly frustrated and discontented heart.

Commit your life and your desires to God. Then watch him fill your life. The inevitable overflow will refresh the lives of others.

3

INGENUITY BY THE BARRELFUL

Dresses, shoes, blouses, skirts, teakettle, shoe polish, pots and pans, pictures — the list, in its own cheerfully jumbled fashion, goes on and on and on.

Books, Christmas decorations, cutlery, camera, hammer and saw (well, there might not be a handy carpenter on the station you are assigned to, and besides it was given to you), aspirin —

Aspirin! Now there's something that could be put to good use immediately. Talk about headaches! You're halfway through the "Suggested Outfit List," and already you're feeling the need to charter an entire ship. Last night it was after midnight before you staggered away from the pile and rolled into bed. You're exhausted; so is your outfit fund.

Going to the mission field had sounded so simple.

You thought all the complications belonged to *being* a missionary, not in getting to your destination.

The days, the weeks, and even the months pass without any slackening of the pace: packing, buying, repacking, and then packing some more. Your head whirls as you try to get together all the things you will need. If you are short of stature, a sore tummy may add to your agonies. How else does one fill the bottom of a barrel except by balancing on the rim with feet swinging raffishly in the air?

Really! Are all these things necessary to being a missionary? Believe it or not, the answer to that question is "yes." You'll be amazed to discover the effect the contents of those barrels will have on your missionary life.

As a single girl, you may never have had a home of your own. If you've been a career girl, you may have had an apartment but probably spent very little time in it. After all, why sit at home alone when there are concerts to attend, young people's get-togethers, and weekend trips with, or to, friends and family. Cooking? No problem. There were boxes, cans, bottles, ready-to-brown rolls, TV dinners, and just about any ready-made goody you could want. If you wanted atmosphere as well as a good meal, you had a favorite restaurant.

On the field your spare time will be spent very differently. Go prepared to center a good deal of your relaxation time around your home.

What is a single missionary's home for? What is any home for? If you had a happy home, you will know the truth of the words "Every house where love abides and friendship is a guest is surely home;

and home, sweet home, for there the heart can rest."

Don't counter with, "But I am just a single girl. It takes a husband and children to make a real home." Do you remember a certain home outside Jerusalem in the little town of Bethany? It was a home Jesus loved to visit when he was near Jerusalem. It seemed to have everything — real love, friendship, and the refreshment of gracious hospitality. Perhaps one of the things he enjoyed more than anything else was the fact that he could relax there. It was a place where he could be away from the crowds and from the constant treachery of the scribes and Pharisees. (Did you ever wonder what the guest room must have been like in that home? Whatever else was put there for his comfort, I have a feeling that there was always a fresh bouquet of flowers in a lovely, well-chosen vase.)

Mother, father, and children? No. Just two sisters and a brother who knew what the elements of a real home were. Mary and Martha knew how to dispense true hospitality. How much it meant to the Savior!

It is just as important for a single girl as it is for a family to have a real home on the field. You won't want to live unto yourself; happiness is always to be found in serving others. Besides, hospitality is not just a nicety; it is a Christian virtue. Paul exhorted, "Practice hospitality." Plan to make your home or apartment attractive and pleasant, so it will say by its very appearance, "You're welcome here." It will not only be a distinct asset to your happiness; it will be a definite aid to your ministry.

Just what things might help make your missionary home life a satisfaction to you and a blessing to others? There is no need to discuss basic furniture. You know you need a bed, a table, a chair, and cupboards. Your mission will advise when and where to get these essentials. Let us concentrate on the extras — the things that you may not have thought were very important. In fact, you have perhaps thought some of them were luxuries that missionaries shouldn't even think about.

When you start selecting things, pick a color scheme. You may be buying some things, and friends will no doubt be asking you what you want or need. Most people prefer that you be specific; they won't think you are being too choosy if you mention your color scheme. It may not work, but you can always try. And it will make a real difference in the general appearance of your apartment.

If possible, find out what general type of living quarters you will have. If you will be living with another girl, try to correspond with her. Try to find out what the windows will be like — big, small, long and narrow, short and wide. Unless you know the size of windows, don't buy ready-made curtains. Get fabric. If you will be in an area where good fabrics are available at a reasonable price, wait until you get to the field to cope with curtains.

Don't leave any nice things at home that you may have already acquired. You'll wish a hundred times you had them on the field. I'm thinking of cut-glass goblets, a beautiful vase, or a party dress. Don't go out and buy expensive things but don't leave them at home if you already have them. How many missionaries I have heard say, "I wish I had brought my —"

If you are going to be hospitable, you'll need dishes for more than two. How many should you get? Believe it or not, you'll find a set for at least eight very useful. They don't have to be expensive to be nice. I have a set of unusually-designed ceramic dishes — service for fourteen — that cost me thirty-one dollars.

The age of plastic dishes has been hailed a godsend for missionaries. Some of us don't agree. It is nice to have a few plastics for everyday use and picnicking, but they aren't necessarily the best for everything. Even the best-looking and most expensive plastic dishes scar, stain, and lose their finish. You can get an inexpensive set of pottery that will look nicer than plastic for a longer period of time.

"But," you say, "pottery will break, and I'm going to have native help." Well, as suggested, have some plastic dishes around for everyday use. If you can't teach your native help to be careful, then do your good dishes yourself when you have company. It might be good practice for furlough time. You'll be drying dishes (or you should be) in every home you visit.

A single missionary I know took a large set of lovely Japanese china to the bush country of Africa years ago. As far as I know, they are still intact (and she has native help).

Other accessories for the table are nice and don't have to be expensive either. On one furlough I bought six tall, imitation milkglass vases for eighty-

eight cents. They double as candle holders. Often
I arrange them with four as candle holders and
two as vases, with a couple of roses in each.

Many countries are great for their coffee-and-tea
parties. It is delightful and helpful to have something special for these occasions. Over the years
I've collected a number of bone china tea cups.
How they have been used — and not only for special tea parties! Tea is wonderful in them, even when
there is only you to enjoy it.

Be sure to find out about the type of lighting on
the field to which you are going. You will want to
take lamps for your home. You can get cheaper
and nicer ones, in most cases, in North America,
although with some ingenuity, you can *make* lamps
to fit the country and your home. Big brass can-
dlesticks, driftwood, clay pots, and big bottles make
wonderful lamps. At least consider your lighting.
Even nice kerosene lamps are available at home, if
you won't have electricity on your field.

Lamp shades of any kind are hard to pack. If
you can't pack them suitably, think about taking
lamp shade kits. Many different kinds are available.

There are a few common kitchen utensils which
may be difficult, if not impossible, to obtain in the
country to which you are going. Most countries
have different ways of measuring food stuffs than
we do (if indeed they measure them at all). Be
sure to take a good supply of measuring cups and
spoons. Take a good egg beater; the ones with ny-
lon gears are the best. You'd be surprised how
hard it is to find a rotary egg beater outside of

North America. Put in a good knife sharpener. You'll always thank yourself for that.

For basic baking utensils, try to take two pie plates, two layer-cake pans, a loaf pan, two sets of muffin tins (you'll be surprised how much you'll use these), two cookie sheets, and a 9-by-13-inch cake pan. Add a tube pan if you can. It is best to get a good grade of aluminum, unless you want and can afford stainless steel. Coated metal pans rust very quickly.

It isn't necessary to have many cooking pots and skillets, but do try to take good heavy ones, either aluminum or stainless steel. Have at least one big pot for company cooking. One covered casserole dish will come in very handy too. By all means try to take a pressure cooker or pressure sauce pan, not only because of the time it saves, but because you may land in a part of the world that doesn't specialize in tender meat.

What about cookbooks? Our modern cookbooks look as delicious as we hope the food tastes. But have you ever read one, keeping in mind the limitations of the country in which you will live? Notice how many recipes call for a can of this or a package of that — marshmallows, chocolate chips, graham crackers, peanut butter, biscuit mix, cake flour, pudding and jello mixes. "Roll it in crushed corn flakes," "use blended spices," "wrap it in aluminum foil," "protect it with wax paper," "dry it between paper towels." These and a hundred-and-one other details, which wouldn't cause a second thought at home, suddenly create problems.

In many cities you can get at least some of these

items. But they will be more expensive than at
home, and your missionary allowance will surely
be less than the budget to which you are accus-
tomed. In most of the so-called primitive areas of
the world, you simply cannot get our common kitchen commodities.

Usually the main difference in basic cooking or
baking ingredients between North America and
other countries is the flour. At home you are used
to powder-dry flour. Elsewhere, it is nearly always
coarser and wetter. You will just have to experi-
ment with the flour until you learn the right quan-
tities, since no doubt you will end up using foreign flour in North American recipes.

There is one thing you can do as far as cookbooks are concerned. Try to get some that were
published earlier than 1950. The flour used in
North America thirty years ago is much closer to
what you can expect to find elsewhere. Also,
the older books do not call for prepared foods. I
brought with me a cookbook published by a wom-
en's missionary federation in a farming community
in the western states. The first edition was published in 1937. I rarely use any other cookbook
now, because this one is so well suited for foreign
baking ingredients. I have a few new cookbooks
with colorful pictures. I occasionally drag them
out, drool over them, and get ideas from them, but
I nearly always use the old one for baking or fol-
lowing a complete recipe.

How about those kitchen commodities? Can't
you take them with you, or can't some one send
them to you from time to time? You can; it's been

done before. But if you make up your mind to live
on the foods available in the country to which you
are assigned (barring, of course the basics we are
used to or are necessary for your health), you'll
find the challenge fun. Besides, you will have more
money for other things, and your friends and family at home will be able to spend their money in
better ways too.

It is nice to have some home foodstuffs as a real
treat now and then, but some girls simply depend
on packages from home. I know one girl who, after almost three years on the field, still hadn't baked
a cake from scratch. Cake mixes are heavy items to
send across the ocean regularly.

When I pack for the field I generally include about
twenty-five dollars worth of flavoring, jellos, wax paper, aluminum foil, plastic wrap, cupcake papers,
and birthday cake candles. I consider the last item
to be one of real value. (I have a cheap cake dec-
orator set, and I could not possibly count the number of birthday cakes I have made and decorated
for adults since being on the field. They never fail
to bring real pleasure.) These things, along with the
small Christmas boxes from home, are rationed
over the period of four to five years on the field.
Even so, certain flavorings are about the only things
for which it is really difficult or impossible to find
substitutes where I am.

I am a hotcake, or pancake, fan and serve them
often, even to guests. So I take a lot of maple
flavoring for maple syrup and also use it as a substitute for other flavors.

I make more chocolate chip cookies than any

other kind, but I never use chocolate chips — not the prepared variety, at least. The substitute, chopped bittersweet chocolate bars, is wonderful, especially since you can make the chocolate pieces as big as you like.

Another major consideration for those barrels will be your wearing apparel. No matter what the mission outfit list says and no matter what you think you'll need, when you get to the field there are some things you'll wish you had done differently. You are a fortunate girl if you have learned to sew. However, even if you hate the thought of sewing or can't sew, try to swallow your "I just can't do it" attitude. Take along some pieces of material and even a sewing machine if you possibly can. Include a sewing instruction book. After two or three years on the field you'll be saying, "If only I had a new dress to wear — mine are so faded, and since I've lost (or gained) so much weight, nothing fits me." Then you will have the impetus necessary to conquer the sewing machine. Start with a very simple pattern, and you'll find it creative and fun, and far less difficult than you thought it would be.

I take practically my entire wardrobe to the field in the form of material. My weight fluctuates so much on furlough that it simply is not practical either to buy or make much while home. Another consideration is that you can make four to six nice dresses for the price you often have to pay for one in a store. I am not an expert seamstress. In fact, I try to keep anyone from examining my workmanship too closely, especially the zippers and buttonholes. But I still consider the struggle to be well worthwhile and get a lot of enjoyment out of seeing and wearing the finished product.

Where does one find time to sew? Did you ever notice that you always seem to have time for the things that you really want to do? I know one missionary girl who pulls out a piece of material and makes a dress when she gets upset about something. She sews furiously, and for her, it's a marvelous emotional release. She has several dresses she calls her "mad" dresses. (No comment on her reason for making the dress!) But it is a good illustration of what I'm trying to say. Sewing is a good creative outlet for a woman, as well as of real practical value.

Another important consideration is your shoes. No matter what the outfit list may say, be sure to bring some shoes suitable for hiking. If you are going to bush country, naturally you will think of it. But if you are going to a big city area, the idea may not occur to you. Tennis shoes are good, as well as something a bit more substantial.

You may not have done much walking at home. You are almost sure to do more on the field. You'll probably learn to appreciate the out-of-doors very much, even if you didn't while you were at home. Both physical and spiritual strains can be lessened if you learn to appreciate every available source of beauty. It may be a desert flower in a very barren country or a beautiful sunset over sand dunes. It may be a lush jungle with its exotic flowers and vines, or mountains and streams. It may even be a tiny patch of green in the middle of a city. Whatever it is, it can be a source of refreshment

resulting in adoration and praise to your Heavenly
Father. It's amazing how a walk in the open air
can lift your soul from the daily tasks that threaten
at times to close in on you.

Think seriously before you go to the field about
what you will do for relaxation. It is important.
You may think that you will have no time to relax
as a missionary — you hardly have time to sleep
at home. That probably will not be the case. You
will *need* relaxation. And you may actually find
you have more spare time on the field than at home.
Life moves at a much slower pace in most of the
world than it does in North America. You may
find that your evenings drag out in silence, whether
you're alone or with another girl.

It is important, I think, to take along something
for good listening. Consider seriously a good tape
recorder or a record player. They are a big help
against loneliness and depression, especially if you
appreciate music at all. I find my tape recorder
good company while I do my housework and as
background for writing all those letters to supporters and friends and family.

It is nice, too, to have a tape recorder for making tapes to send home. There is nothing like being
able to talk occasionally to those at home rather
than writing a letter. The folks at home love re-
ceiving live word. Also, many missionaries find
tape recorders a real aid to language study.

Before you buy any kind of recording equipment
or record player, be sure to consult someone who
knows (not just an outspoken amateur). Find out
what is the best kind of equipment to take to the

area to which you are going. Climate is a big consideration, especially if you are heading for the tropics. And don't forget the type of power you will be using on your field. If there is no electricity, you will need battery-powered equipment. Many of these run on inexpensive and readily-available flashlight batteries. Someone already on your field can recommend a type or brand of equipment.

Take as many good books as possible with you, including a good variety. Missionary biographies will be a real source of encouragement to you. Take the books you already have, even if you have read them. They will be more useful than you think — either to you or to someone else. Build up your personal library as much as your funds will permit. Paperbacks are wonderful. You can have so much good reading material for so little cost and save weight too!

Even though you may not particularly like, or have time for, table games and jigsaw puzzles at home, take at least a small selection of them with you. Sooner or later you'll find them a real aid to your social life.

The more you can provide your own relaxation and entertainment, the less of a burden you will be on fellow missionaries when you are a little bored, lonely, or in need of a lighter touch to life. This is vital particularly if you will be stationed with only one other girl and one or two families.

Cameras. What can be said to convince you of the value of taking good pictures with a good camera? If you have a camera at home and like to take pictures, then you will have discovered its value already. But many single girls do not fall into that category. Either they just don't want to be bothered with taking pictures, or they think that cameras are too complicated. Others may consider it a man's hobby.

Besides the joy of being able to share a bit of what you see with those at home, slides are a must for deputation work. How else can you communicate a completely different culture and way of life to those who have never been farther from home than the next town or state or province? People want to visualize where you live and what you do. You undoubtedly learned in school that seeing as well as hearing creates a far bigger impact on the mind and heart than hearing alone.

But gone are the days when just any old slides will do. The people at home will expect to see *good* pictures, not fuzzy, out-of-focus, blurred ones. Can you blame them? How many times have you been bored and exasperated by some of the slide presentations church groups are forced to suffer through in the name of missionary spirit?

There is no reason why people should not see good pictures of your work — even if you have never taken pictures before. Exposures are not so complicated when you buy a camera with an automatic exposure device. There are many good, relatively inexpensive cameras of this type on the market now, such as the instamatic variety. With some you don't even have to thread the film. You just insert a cartridge, close the back, and start shooting pictures.

When you see a picture you especially like — one

that reaches your heart — ask yourself what makes the picture effective, and then remember the reason. Talk to someone who knows photography, and ask for a few tips. Also buy a simple instruction book that gives the basics of taking good pictures. Good pictures are important!

Before you stand on the lid of that last barrel, think about one more thing: Christmas. No matter what the season may have meant to you at home, it will mean more in a foreign land.

How can the awesome message of Christmas — "Joy to the world, the Lord is come!" — help but mean more to you in a land which has experienced little or nothing of Christ's redeeming love? The songs of Christmas will thrill you more than ever before. I've found great urge on the field to make things "Christmasy" around the apartment. It seems, too, that everyone else enjoys the atmosphere.

However, Christmas seems to be a time when many missionaries, especially single ones, feel left out and homesick. I have heard more than one single girl say rather dismally on her first Christmas on the field, "I'm not going to do much. Christmas just isn't Christmas without family or children around." It isn't? Since when did Christmas belong only to families or to children? We've allowed the commercial slant of the season to spoil the real meaning of the time for us.

When you are packing those barrels, remember Christmas. If you are going to a place where trees or tree substitutes are not available, tuck an artificial tree into your barrel. Even nice ones are

cheap enough these days. Include some other types
of decorations, too. Why not include some lights
if you will have electricity on your field? The tradi-
tional Christmas tree candles are nice too. And a
bit of Christmas paper and ribbon won't break your
pocketbook, but it will bring somebody a lot of
cheer. The nationals will probably love it too.

These suggestions were not meant to be a complete
list. The essentials are conspicuously absent. The
suggestions are meant to be just that — suggestions
to guide your thinking on some of the extras which
will be of real value to you as a single missionary.

Perhaps you think that they are all a bit superflu-
ous. If so, you may spend a lot of time during
your first term deciding what to bring back next
time!

4

SELECTED FOR DISCIPLESHIP

Servitude Department
Course 101 — (3 hours credit): How to Be a Servant

Eye trouble? You might have good reason to suspect it if you ever saw that entry in the catalogue of a Christian college or Bible school. A great deal of time is spent teaching future Christian leaders how to be leaders for God and how to use their abilities and talents for him. Most of the training is very good. But here's the paradox. Most graduates (myself included) embark as teachers, pastors, and missionaries having learned at least in theory how best to serve God with the tools we have. We haven't learned, though, how to be servants.

What does it mean to be a servant of God? What does it mean to be a servant? Whatever else it may mean, being a servant means learning to live and work under authority.

For our rebellious human natures, that is not easy, especially if that authority tells us to do something we don't want to do. This kind of learning doesn't come out of a textbook. It has to be learned by experience, sometimes hard experience.

The army, for example, has to teach men and women how to live under authority. It's the first item on the training schedule for the new recruit. For some recruits, it's very difficult. A few never learn. But the army will not take excuses, or even reasons, for lack of obedience to a command.

Can you imagine a fellow who has been on the battlefront for a few weeks marching up to his commanding officer with: "Look here! I speak the native language fluently. I want a little responsibility with the intelligence group. I'm not going to spend my time digging trenches." Could anyone get away with saying, "I was trained to be a high school teacher; I'm not going to load ammunition"? Or this from a private: "Sarge, I'm afraid we'll have to stop the war early this afternoon. I've got a date for dinner tonight, and I really need some time to get ready."

Even this spurt of well-meant enthusiasm wouldn't go over: "I joined the Army because I thought it was the patriotic thing to do! Sort of like a calling. You want me to drive a what? A truck? No, sir! I'm not going to drive any truck. I came to do something important, not drive some dirty old truck. I want to see action." Or, "Sorry to be late for the war, General. The barracks needed new curtains, and there wasn't any important fighting to do today, was there?"

Could these snatches of conversation ever be heard in an army? In a regular army, no. In the army of the Lord —? How many excuses have you made to stay out of the battle? We take servitude — living under authority — for granted in the army of our government. Can we do any less in God's army?

Learning to live under authority may disturb you a great deal. When you land on the mission field and are asked to fill in for the office odd-job girl while she's home on furlough, you may hardly be able to conceal your disappointment. You may feel like crying out, "But that isn't what I came to do. I spent four years and a lot of money training to be a missionary, and you want me to baby-sit a file cabinet, run a mimeograph, be a stamp licker?" You might feel as if you can't even write home and tell your supporters what you are doing. After all, they expect you to be out winning the heathen!

Perhaps you have a college degree and expected to be teaching native workers in the Bible school. Instead you find yourself teaching in a missionary children's school and playing part-time mother.

Why aren't things the way the mission board told you they would be? Why must you mark time doing what seem to be insignificant tasks, when you itch to be on the front lines?

There may be some good reasons, some of which you won't find it easy to face.

— Often it is very difficult to envision from home what your situation will be on the field.

— It is difficult for any mission board to know exactly how you will fit into a field situation.

— Emergency conditions often arise, requiring a change in original plans.

— That new ministry they told you about may have met complications in getting under way.

— Perhaps you are having a bad case of culture shock, whether you want to admit it or not.

But, apart from any human reason why you may be doing what you don't want to do, there is a perfect purpose in the mind of your Heavenly Father — the one to whom you laid out your total commitment. You said to him (if your commitment was complete), "Wherever you want me to go; whatever you want me to be." Not only is it his divine right to test your commitment, what kind of commitment would it be if it wasn't tested? It certainly wouldn't mean very much to you.

The difference between obedience in an earthly army and God's army is your motive for living under authority. A man may be inducted into an earthly army against his will. You are motivated in God's army, not by fear of punishment or even by patriotism, but by love for God.

The whole test of your commitment is a proof of your love of God. One measure of your love for him often lies in what you are willing to do for him against your human desires. Or the test may be in not using what you wanted to use in the way of talent, training, or ability.

What about that talent, or even your training, that you so badly wanted the Lord to use? There is sometimes a reason why the Lord seems to have laid aside your talents or disregarded your training that you spent so much time and effort and expense to acquire. Perhaps it means so much to you personally that unless the Lord lays it aside, at least for a time, he cannot be glorified in it.

Why does God give us talents, anyway? *The Living Bible* paraphrase of Ephesians 4:12 puts it this way: "Why is it that he gives us these special abilities to do certain things best? It is that God's people will be equipped to do better work for him — building up the church, the body of Christ, to a position of strength and maturity."

That pretty well packs the story into a nutshell, doesn't it? If God can't utilize your talent or training to build up the Church, don't expect him to use it at all. If the temptation to employ your talent or training for self-glory is too great, God may have to put it in the background, perhaps permanently. Are you willing for that?

Perhaps you thought your talent was completely yielded to him. But only the Lord knows the point in your spiritual progress at which you have really let go of it and can honestly say, "If the Lord never chooses to enlist either my talent or my training, then it is all right with me." The Lord cannot use them until they are totally his, not yours. Nor would you be his servant if you reserved the right to make the best use of them. Perhaps by your actions you have asked God to be your servant.

Only as God can try the motives of your commitment can he teach you what it means to be his servant. What is your motive?

Being a servant of God meant much to the Apostle Paul. "What things I had, I counted loss for Christ!" were his words. What did he have? More intelligence, more schooling, higher social standing than most of us would experience in three lifetimes. Yet he counted them as trash in order that he might experience the death of the cross, the fellowship of Christ's sufferings. Love for the Lord was his only motive. What he had was less than nothing in his eyes, so great was his love for his Master. For Christ had become a servant unto death in order to save Paul, the self-avowed chief of sinners.

For Christ, being a servant meant that "though he was in the form of God, [he] did not count equality with God a thing to be grasped, but emptied himself, taking the form of a servant, being born in the likeness of men. And being found in human form he humbled himself and became obedient unto death, even death on a cross" (Philippians 2:6-8 RSV).

That is going all the way! What was his motive? It was love and obedience to his Heavenly Father and love for a world of sinners. How does that compare with your motive?

There is another reason why training and talents may not be used as we would like them to be — a reason that can be a little hard on the pride. Despite your training, perhaps you're not as profi-

cient as someone told you you were or as you may
have imagined. Some missionaries have trained
themselves for specific jobs or spent years developing what they thought was a real talent. They
arrived on the field and didn't have a chance to
use their training or talent for one reason. They
simply were not good enough to fill the require-
ments for the position.

Certainly it takes all the grace the Lord can give
to face that. But don't blame the mission. Remember, they usually have only the references of
well-wishing friends and pastors to go on. The
mission might even have tested you out a bit and
still mistakenly overrated your abilities.

If that sounds difficult to accept, it is. It is one
of the hardest things a missionary may have to face.
But you can trust the God who led you to the field
to put you in a position of most complete value to
him and richest fulfillment in your personal life.

Perhaps you will find God will use your ability;
perhaps he will ask you to bury it. Either way,
when you let him make the decision, he will lead
you to ministries of which you may not have
dreamed. And the result will certainly be a most
satisfying relationship to him and to others around
you.

What makes you want to be a missionary? What
makes you want to be a servant of the Lord?
What drives you on? The drive to give your life,
your talents, your abilities? Do you see yourself
working, teaching, wearing yourself out for him?
Perhaps you will wear yourself out. It has happened to many others before you. The Lord may

strip you of your natural resources — your health and strength. He may permit you to wear yourself out until your nerves are tight and raw, until just the effort to think is exhausting. The process is often painful and slow. But he may have to allow it to convince you that you are nothing, that you have no ability or strength of your own. If you really want to be a true servant, he will have to show you, perhaps through deep personal suffering, that love for him needs to be your only motive and to glorify God your only goal.

Remember what great things Paul accomplished for his Lord, how many souls he won for his Savior, how many churches he founded? And yet it was the same Paul whose only ambition was "to really know Christ and to experience the mighty power that brought him back to life again, and to find out what it means to suffer and die with him" (Philippians 3:10 TLB). Is that *your* goal, *your* only ambition?

Of course, for all of us, it's a continuing process. Paul went on, "I don't mean to say I am perfect. I haven't learned all I should even yet, but I keep working toward that day when I will finally be all that Christ saved me for and wants me to be."

There is another circumstance that may keep you in the background for awhile. Sometimes, unfortunately, senior missionaries are jealous of a junior's abilities. It's hard to put that on paper, but it does happen. Missionaries are human too. Can you suffer wrong? Can you still ask God to give you the grace and love you need to remain in the background silently and graciously, perhaps even at menial tasks, until the time he chooses to allow your abilities to shine? Remember Joseph? What we do or what we have really isn't that important to the Lord. He is interested in what we are.

Paul made an honest appraisal of his own importance. "Whatever gain I had, I counted as loss for the sake of Christ. Indeed I count everything as loss because of the surpassing worth of knowing Christ Jesus my Lord. For his sake I have suffered the loss of all things, and count them as refuse, in order that I may gain Christ . . . (Philippians 3:7 RSV).

It seems Paul didn't worry when the church council didn't properly appreciate his educational training. He apparently didn't mind making tents now and then. In fact, he probably enjoyed it. Are you content to be a tent maker?

What about David? If you recall, he spent many years in the background, a fugitive fleeing in the wilderness. That was after he had been anointed king. He had opportunities to get rid of the opposition; he could have stepped out and claimed his rightful place. But, instead, he went out of his way to show respect and love to Saul.

David had close friends "in the mission" who could have aided him. Few friendships have been more committed than the one he had with Jonathan. Many of the loyal men with him would gladly have stirred up Israel to rebel against Saul so David could possess the kingdom.

If David could trust God to vindicate him, you can too. Don't molest God's servant who is over you, either by word or deed or thought. Instead, pray desperately for him or her and the situation daily. It will amaze you to see how the Lord can solve the situation in his own way. Maybe he will change *you* to fit the situation!

If you ask the Lord to keep you from forcing your hand into the circumstance, you will be richly blessed and a great deal happier to have seen God work it out his way. And God will honor you for it, as he most certainly did David.

David's character and personality certainly were strengthened by his humiliation and suffering. It was a rich time of becoming conformed to the image of the God he loved and to whom he was so faithful. Your tribulations can do the same for you.

When God gets ready to use you, he will. In the meantime, let him make you a true servant of God.

5

COEXISTENCE OR COMPANIONSHIP?

Elaine stood in the doorway, rigid with hurt. Confusion and anger tensed the muscles of her stomach. The field chairman's face blurred crazily across her vision as she fought back the tears that threatened to break over her eyelashes.

"Elaine!" exclaimed Mr. Swanson. "Whatever is wrong?"

"It's JoAnne — you've simply got to — please — I — I can't live with her another day!" With that the flood of tears broke loose down her deeply-tanned cheeks and splashed onto the cement threshold below. There. It was out. And with the release of pent-up emotion, a sense of stupidity, embarrassment, and shame settled over her. For a full minute she stood there, overcome with the emotion that tore at her.

When the flood had subsided Mr. Swanson invited, a bit flatly: "Come in and sit down. Perhaps we can talk about it."

Seated across from him, Elaine stammered: "I'm sorry. I've — I guess I've made a mess of things. I've tried to like JoAnne. Honestly. I know it's a terrible thing to have to admit, especially when I'm a missionary, but I just can't like her. Can't something be done?" she implored. "I can't think. I can't pray. I can't teach or do anything right, I'm so upset. And I'm afraid JoAnne is in the same boat. We can't seem to open our mouths without annoying each other."

The words tumbled out one on top of the other. They made no particular sense and Elaine knew it. She also knew that there really wasn't anything Mr. Swanson could do about it, at least, not at the moment. There wasn't another place on the compound for her or JoAnne to live. Besides, it seemed very silly to think that the mission could, or would, spend money to build another apartment just to resolve a personality clash.

Her mind snapped back to the room to hear Mr. Swanson reminding her: "I'm sorry, Elaine, but my hands are tied. You know there is no other place for either of you to live. You also know that JoAnne is not the type of girl who can live alone. You are both important to the work. Please ask the Lord to help you."

Elaine rose without another word and left. Her steps dragged reluctantly back across the compound to the bungalow she and JoAnne shared. Suddenly the song the choir had sung on the night she had committed her life to Christ flooded through her memory: "I'll go with him, with him, all the way." Somehow the excited thrill of that commitment had flattened out into a dull, solid-gray drudgery. In the year she had been on the field, she had little to show for her life but a frustrated spirit. It was all because of JoAnne; at least, that is what she told herself. Didn't the Lord understand? Didn't he know what having to live with JoAnne was doing to her?

Why did she have to live with another girl anyway? The Lord could have called Rick, too. It would have made it so much easier to be an effective missionary.

For a long moment, self-pity burned in her frustrated heart. When she reached the door, she stepped inside almost on tiptoe. She couldn't bear the thought of an encounter with JoAnne at the moment. She slipped into her room and quietly closed the door behind her. Once again the tears began to flow. She sank to her knees, her head buried in the blue chintz bedspread.

Elaine is not the only one who has shed tears over the problem of a roommate. It has happened all through the last two centuries of foreign missions. Unfortunately, there are no "ready-mix" instant answers. The problem of a roommate remains a problem.

On the surface the situation looks ideal: there is somebody for friendship, someone to pray with, a partner in the ministry, somebody to spend spare time with, and two people to do the cooking and household chores — a real time-saver.

Why does it so often not work smoothly? One of the simplest answers is that, humanly speaking, a woman was not made to share the responsibility of a home with another woman. She likes to cook and entertain *her* way. She has her own household time schedule. She has fixed ideas about the way the furniture should be arranged. She doesn't need help from another woman to decide that. If she is married, she can be pretty sure her husband won't balk at the way she has arranged the furniture (that is, unless she did it while he was at work, and upon returning home after dark he falls over an armchair he didn't know was there). She can be fairly sure that her husband will not only let her keep the house and do the cooking the way she likes, but that he'll take pride in her for it. At very best, living with another girl is a substitute for the real thing.

So there you are — a successfully run household doesn't need both a supervisor and a straw boss. But saying it isn't very workable doesn't solve the problems that flourish when it becomes necessary for two naturally imcompatible personalities to live and run a household together.

Are there no answers? Must we continually see girls living a good share of their missionary life in spiritual defeat and frustration because of incompatibilities in their home? Some grow bitter and sarcastic, unable to carry on a conversation without barbs; some develop a sense of bondage while living with a domineering girl; some are weighed down with a girl who is too dependent; others are burdened by jealous roommates or ones who are too attached to them.

There is more than one reason why single missionary girls often *should* live together. The first of course is financial. In many cases, it would be a waste of the Lord's money to buy, build, or rent two separate dwelling places so that we can have our own selfish feminine way about things.

Furthermore, many cultures put a big question mark over girls who live alone. In a situation like that, to avoid what is to the nationals the appearance of evil, girls *must* not live alone.

Many girls need and want companionship. They would rather share an apartment with another girl than live alone. Unfortunately, they often end up with a girl who doesn't feel the same about it.

Does God intend for you to heave a sigh of resignation and accept your roommate problems with "This is my cross and I guess I'll just have to carry it"? Does he mean for you to "grin and bear it" and end up distracted and frustrated? Does God make a habit of calling people to his work and then dumping them into impossible situations that they must spend the rest of their lives attempting to endure?

No. There are some practical things you can do. The rest must then be left to the Lord to take care of.

Be aware of potential problems at the outset. Sometimes bad precedents are set at the beginning which the girls were afraid to break later for fear of hurt feelings. It is the old proverb: "An ounce of prevention is worth a pound of cure." In this type of relationship it really holds true.

Try to learn your roommate's background as quickly as possible. Showing a warm interest in it will take you a long way toward knowing what makes her tick. You may be much less ready to condemn her when you realize what she has had to overcome.

Household matters cause as much problem as anything. Discuss these very clearly and in detail at the very beginning. Most girls alternate household tasks — cooking, cleaning, and shopping. In some cases there may be local help, but even then it may be convenient to alternate time periods for instructing the help. That is better than expecting the help to take orders from two people at once.

When it is your roommate's turn to cook or clean, stay out of her way. If the way she peels potatoes, makes pie crust, or messes up the kitchen makes you nervous — stay out. It will help you both. Even if there is an easier, neater, faster, better way of doing things, even if the biscuits would turn out better if she did them your way, keep your mouth closed. She may ask your advice after eating your productions. Even then, give it sparingly and courteously with words of encouragement. Don't rattle off the instructions with the smugness of a professional. If she doesn't follow your instructions — don't mention it.

It is best, I believe, to make the rule that whoever does the cooking cleans the kitchen too. In that way there should be no problems between the immaculate housekeeper and the disorganized "messer" on that score.

If, despite all your efforts to keep the apartment

clean, she messes it up and leaves things thrown around constantly, ask the Lord to give you grace. After all, does it matter in the final analysis if her skirt is over the back of the chair in the living room where she left it when she slipped out of it last night? Is the world going to fall apart? If someone comes and sees it there, so what? Usually they'll know whose it is and, even if they don't, is it worth frustrated spirits, defeated hearts, and hindered ministries? If it is, it is time for a long, hard look at yourself. You just might find some selfish pride there.

Then there is the question of sharing household expenses. This again is sticky, or it can be. It takes more than rules and general agreements. It often takes a strong grasp on the grace of God, especially if a penny-pincher and an undisciplined spender have been thrown together. Often the "pincher" is proud of her frugality and the spender of her generosity.

Most girls have a kitty, or common general account, for the household funds. Discuss it very frankly and openly when you start living together. Some just match funds in it, and when it is out, add more. Some agree to stick to a budget. Try especially to meet each other halfway on your ideas of entertaining. That takes the biggest extras out of the kitty, especially for single girls. A family of five doesn't notice the financial drain of having another family of five over for dinner nearly as much as a single girl notices the deficit in her housekeeping fund after feeding five people.

If you have to spend a few more pennies, or even

dollars, than you would if you were alone, don't begrudge them. Ask the Lord to make you a cheerful contributor to the well-being of your household. He will no doubt reward you for it.

If you find it absolutely impossible to agree on how to spend your money or what kind of a diet to have, as a last resort and after much prayer and careful consideration of your situation with your roommate, try living separately in your apartment. The outcome depends a lot on how you broach the subject and what your attitude is when you talk about it. Be open and frank and appreciative of the other's views.

I would say that to live separately in the same apartment could not work, except for one reason: I have seen it succeed beautifully. The two girls I am thinking of had separate places in the cupboard for their utensils, spices, and foods. When one wanted to entertain and the other didn't, the one who didn't just stayed in her room and out of the way. Sometimes they did entertain together. There was a frankness, consideration, freedom, and real friendship in their situation. I marveled at it and thought, "Why don't more try it?" After all, that is the way many working girls live who have different interests and schedules. It is not at all an impossible situation, especially if you've tried it with an open heart and before trouble really brews and has made bitter hearts.

Except perhaps in an unusual circumstance, it is best not to have joint ownership of anything. You aren't husband and wife, and no matter how permanent your situation may look to you, it probably isn't. If you don't own anything together, you won't have to worry about what to do with things when you part company. You might both want the same article, or the one who is left with it may not feel that the particular item is worth spending money on to pay for the other's half-interest.

It is especially important not to have joint ownership of a car. One is bound to be a better driver than the other. Who pays in case of an accident? If you ride together and want to share gas and oil expenses, that is different. But if you own the car and the other gal is a poor driver, you can feel perfectly free to let her know, in a nice way, who does the driving.

When you own a car together, there's the question of who gets it if you need to go in different directions at the same time. Joint ownership sometimes creates a real sense of bondage when girls want to be considerate. They're always afraid they may be overusing it and monopolizing the benefits.

There are ways of preventing foreseen trouble. Even so, don't become too attached to things. Something may happen to them and it may be your roommate who is to blame. I remember one girl who had a very unmechanical roommate. At different times she plugged her 110-volt iron, tape recorder, and automatic toaster into 220 volts. Result? (If you don't know the answer to that, then you'd better learn the dangers of using incorrect voltage before you leave for the field and the same thing happens to you.) Love and patience? Many times she needed an extra portion from the Lord.

When you discover that your roommate doesn't

like a certain thing, avoid doing it or talking about it in her presence. For instance, if she doesn't like to have her English corrected or doesn't like to be teased about her peculiar accent, don't do it, no matter if you think you'll choke trying to keep your mouth shut.

Don't knowingly torment hot tempers and jealous hearts. Even if they are wrong, you are not right when you deliberately aggravate them. The fact that her temptations are not yours doesn't give you license to exploit hers. In fact, God will hold you accountable for it. Ask the Lord to give you the wisdom and gentleness of Christian consideration.

One girl nearly drove her roommate "up the wall" by playing her radio. She had it on constantly, listening to anything and everything. There just had to be a certain noise level in the background. I can appreciate the nervous frustration of that roommate very much. If there is any annoyance or disagreement over your listening tastes, whether it is the radio, tape recorder, or record player — set it up in your own room and listen to it there, where it won't disturb your roommate.

Unless it is necessary (as in many cases it is), try not to spend your vacation time together. No matter how much you think of each other, no matter how well you get along together, you need a certain amount of time apart. Naturally, for those who have difficulty in living together, it is a great help and refreshment to spend vacations separately. For those who are too attached to each other, it will give fresh perspectives and perhaps even give the Lord a chance to reveal who is wrongfully coming first in their lives.

Though one does not like to even think of an improper physical attachment between missionary girls, it is best to face it as a possibility. Sad to say, tragedies of that nature are not unknown in the mission field.

Sometimes girls are caught in this shameful snare of the devil before they realize what is happening. Perhaps a girl is a lonely, overly-affectionate person. Perhaps a girl just wants to help out someone who has that problem, and gets involved herself. Often these problems, coupled with failure to face one's own flesh as sinful flesh, can spell real calamity.

Probably you would never dream it could happen to you. It won't, if your heart is where it should be before the Lord. But if you feel you have any weakness that way, keep a constant watch before the Lord. If you see in your relationship with another girl even a hint that you are headed in the wrong direction — do something now! Lay it before the Lord. Be sure that he comes first.

You may be going down the wrong path if you feel that your friend is irreplaceable in your life. Perhaps those are not your feelings, but she feels that way about you. Then it is time to be very honest and open with her. Have a firm, frank, gracious talk about the dangers of becoming too close. If she loves the Lord at all, she will agree. If she does not respond, you might have to ask your mission administration for a change. It is a shameful, embarrassing thing to have to uncover, but it is a

million times better to uncover it before it gets to
serious proportions than to wait until it is too late
to do anything but pack up your bags and go home
— heartbroken and knocked out of the Lord's commission.

Apart from a physical relationship, you may find
you need the Lord's help and wisdom to prevent a
mental bondage from developing. This applies especially to those who are, or have, overly-depen-
dent roommates. For instance, there should be
enough freedom between you so that one can be
invited out to dinner without the other — with no
hurt feelings. In these matters be very open. If
you have the attitude that your roommate is going
to be hurt if you do something on your own, she
probably will be. If she *is* hurt, talk lovingly and
openly to her, but don't stop acting independently.

That doesn't mean you may be inconsiderate. It
is not a mark of independence, but of thoughtlessness, to leave for several hours, particularly at
night, and give no clue where you are going or when
you plan to return. I remember being awakened
at one o'clock in the morning by a very worried
single missionary. Her roommate had gone out for
a "little drive" about eight and was not back yet.
My roommate and I both got up and dressed, and
the three of us drove off to search for her. A wild
inspiration finally took us down a dark lane to the
home of some local people with whom we knew she
was friendly. Sure enough, there she was, standing
on the doorstep of the home, talking to the woman
of the house. Her reaction to our concern was
disgust. Her conduct was irresponsible, to say the

very least.

Give your roommate some idea of where you are going, and tell her at least approximately how long you expect to be gone. Besides the fact that it is a good safety precaution for someone always to know where you are, you are bound to inflict hurt if you are secretive about your independent ventures. You both should be independent, but at the same time interested in each other's activities. Face the fact that women in general are curious. There are many ways of avoiding the disclosure of something you really don't want to have her know without being deliberately secretive, which you know will antagonize and hurt. It is amazing, isn't it, how many women are good at dropping just enough information to make a person curious. Somehow it gives them a sense of importance.

"Familiarity breeds contempt" is still a valid truth. Familiarity is a pitfall many girls fall into. It is so subtle that looking back you never can quite understand just where or when or why you or your roommate started taking offense. You tease each other and laugh and then suddenly you discover there is offense. Then the old familiar words, "Oh, come on, I was only teasing," find their way into the conversation. If a girl has a weakness or some peculiar trait, funny as it may seem, deep down she may be very sensitive about it, especially if she views it as an inadequacy. It is always best to try to leave a certain cushion of respectful reserve instead of running things to the ground. It may not be quite as much fun on the surface, but you are sure to remain better friends.

Maintaining a respectful reserve includes politeness too. Don't slide into telling her something that you would like her to do — ask her. Do it with a tone of voice that gives her the right to refuse if she should choose to do so. Be gracious and thankful for what the other one does for you no matter how small it is. It can't be stressed too much how important these little words "please" and "thank you" are. Elementary? Yes, but I know of missionaries who seem never to have put the words into their vocabulary. What a world of difference a little "please" and "thank you" make in relationships with other people, especially when you work and live so close together.

Keep short accounts with your roommate. More harm is done a relationship by refusing to talk over a situation than by anything else. Talk it over completely. Lay out every little item involved before each other, embarrassing as it may be. Misunderstanding is so often at the bottom of an unfortunate situation that comes up. You'll never know that unless you are willing to talk to each other about it.

Women are particularly bad about facing each other with something. They interpret incomplete facts, stories, glances, and silences the way they please. Then they tell them to somebody else as fact. Christian women are as guilty of this as anybody else.

The answer to "Are you sure that is what they meant?" often is, "I don't know, but how could you possibly interpret it any other way?"

"Did you talk to them about it?"

"Of course not! How could I?"

Well, why can't you? Some girls I know have taken an hour and more with a roommate to get to the hidden reason behind a certain situation. Only then did the real feelings come out into the open. But the air was cleared, and all was fine. Is it worth the effort and mental strain? A hundred times over! One girl I know just kept quiet — not a word, sometimes for hours. Though the relationship with her roommate was somewhat improved by the time they parted ways there was always a world of misunderstanding between them.

It may not always be easy to dig out what is eating at your roommate. It may be awkward and embarrassing to try. She may even give you a piece of her mind in the process. In spite of it, ask the Lord to give you the grace you need, the patience, and the humility as you let her know that you are sincerely interested in keeping the air clear between you. You will surely be rewarded.

Try to pray together, even if it is just a short time each day. You don't need to pray together about touchy work situations about which you feel differently. Just kneel and pray together. It is a good time to bear each other's burdens and commit your own relationship to the Lord. You will find that there is one thing this prayer time will do for you — it will really encourage you to keep short accounts with each other. It is difficult to pray together if you do not feel one in spirit.

But when you have done everything you know of, do you still find some situations that seem impossible? For instance — what do you do with a girl who happens to be extremely moody? One day she may favor you with a happy smile or brilliant burst of conversation, but at another time, for seemingly no reason, she will go through a complete meal in silence or even go to her room and shut the door. She may be congenial, or she may clip you so short you feel like an overly-friendly puppy dog who has just had a slap on the nose.

Then there is the girl who is so completely unpredictable that after you have studied her likes and dislikes in an attempt to run parallel with them, you constantly find yourself going enthusiastically at a ninety-degree angle, with an unpleasant surprise waiting at the crossing.

How do you cope with the girl who was a spoiled only-child at home, who never had to lift a finger to help herself? She wanted to be a missionary but had no idea of the manual labor that it entailed. She seems totally unable to do it or perhaps is rebellious at the idea. Or maybe she is so used to having someone wait on her that she doesn't even realize when she is taking advantage of another.

There are almost as many types of problems as there are people. How do you live with problem people without being driven to the ground — and under? The only answer *may* be separation. But there is a great deal to think about before you should ask the mission to consider that step.

Have you asked the Lord to search your heart? Have you asked the Lord to show you how much of the bad temper, jealousy, moodiness, and pettiness come from you? Have you honestly asked God to show you any wrong attitudes in your heart? Have you asked him to break you? Ask him to show you what you are doing to contribute to the tension between you and your roommate.

When the Lord gives you a full look into the sinfulness of your own heart, it is a shattering experience. When you discover how much grace the Lord has shown toward you, it will actually be difficult to heap condemnation on someone else.

Then again, maybe he *has* shown you. Maybe that is your problem. You're only too aware of your temper, your selfishness, your jealousy, and moodiness. You spend many secret hours hating yourself for what you are. You've been honest with God; you've seen yourself as you really are. But that is all you have done. That is as far as you have gone. You've looked in — at you.

The Lord never means for you to stop with your eyes focused inward. He only wants you to look at yourself long enough to know how great his love and grace really is. Then he wants you to look back to him. He wants you to learn the meaning of the most stabilizing truth of your whole Christian life: Jesus Christ is your righteousness!

He is your strength for every task. He is in your every right attitude. He is your love. He is the comfort, the joy, the abounding grace you extend to others. He is your patience. He is your long-suffering. He is your personal confidence. He is your graciousness. He is everything you need. And he is in you, waiting to be what you need. If anything can make you relax in Christ, that ought to. When you fail him — and your roommate — he is your forgiveness.

Do you have an impossible roommate? Or are you one yourself? Before you give up — look in, then look away to Jesus Christ your righteousness.

Don't be surprised if you find yourself wondering what happened to all your roommate problems!

6

FRAGRANT FEMININITY

Independent old-maid missionary! The words bring to mind vivid pictures of fussy old spinsters of the type that can be swallowed only in very small doses.

Men and married couples are not the only ones who shun the old-maid category of missionary. Single girls do too. Girls dread going to the field single for that reason perhaps more than any other. They don't want to be classified with the "typicals."

Deep down, though, most girls don't really mind the outward classification as much as they fear actually joining the category. Some girls seem to be born old maids — as, in a way, some men seem destined for bachelorhood. But many missionary girls fall needlessly into the role. It's easy to do because much of the time a single missionary girl must play a double role.

On deputation she must speak from the pulpit as authoritatively as a man. Often she must set up a projector, and run it, too. It is embarrassing and exasperating to have to do what seems like man's work, especially in front of them. Sometimes it happens because the men don't offer to help and other times because, believe it or not, they simply are not able to. I have carried a heavy movie projector up the aisle, set it up, and threaded and tested it with an audience of men looking on. I have also had to politely tell men who wanted to help, but really didn't know how to go about it, to keep their hands off the expensive film with which I had been entrusted.

My mind is flooded with experiences probably unique to single girl missionaries. One is especially vivid. Burdened with a very heavy suitcase, I got off the bus in a small western town. It was mid-afternoon. The little church where I was scheduled to show a missionary motion picture was a long block away. Of course I walked, and the suitcase wasn't any lighter by the time I arrived. The front door of the little church was open. The situation that met my eyes was, to say the very least, dismaying. In the middle aisle a movie projector had been set up. But what a projector! Ancient was the only word to describe it. For each of its numerous years a layer of dust coated the machine.

I went in search of the pastor. A neighbor informed me that the parsonage was "about eight blocks up that way." So, thanking her, I began the pilgrimage to the parsonage — heavy suitcase and all.

At the parsonage I learned that the pastor had done his best. He had searched everywhere for a projector. Denying him the use of the good one, the high school had offered him an old one from the attic. No one, including the pastor, had a clue how it ran or in what condition it might be. I suggested we should see what we could do with it as soon as possible.

Back at the church, every movable part on the projector was removed and cleaned. I really knew nothing about it myself, since it was only the second time I had operated a movie projector. But I figured that if a part came off it should go on again. Miraculously they all did just that. Sure enough, when we threaded the film and flipped on the switch, there was the delightful image on the screen. But the sound coming from the speaker bore a close resemblance to about a thousand violins playing in frightful discord.

Back to the dismantling and cleaning. Finally we managed to shake some dust out of the sound head (I had no idea if that really was the problem) and gingerly set it up ready to go. I watched the machine like a hawk as people came in, to see that no one jarred the projector.

The meeting began and, preliminaries over, I held my breath as I flicked the switch. There it was in full brilliant color — accompanied by that same discordant screeching. It was obviously not the time for tinkering. I sent up an urgent SOS to my Heavenly Father. He must have been listening for me because it was not the first distress signal sent him that day. Pushing the "off" switch on the sound

track, I narrated the entire film myself — all fifty
minutes of it. Only after it was over did I realize
what a miracle the Lord had performed. Almost
word for word it had come back to me and I had
seen the film only twice before.

That was just one experience. A girl must stand
at the door as people file out, shake their hands,
and give them literature. Often she faces the firing
squad of questioners after the pastor cheerfully in-
vites, "Does anyone have any questions to ask?"
If she does routine secretarial work in a field headquarters or in a large technical missionary opera-
tion, she can find that she is hard put to answer
some of the man-sized questions. (The simplest
answer, by the way, is "I don't know." Don't try
bluffing if you don't know.)

By the time a girl arrives on the field she has done
a herculean job of packing. She has very possibly
roamed through a big freight room full of men,
making sure that the shipment got off without a
problem.

She arrives on the field dead tired. But she is
so used to taking every bull by the horns that she
is apt to forget where she is and that she happens
to be, after all, a lady — a member of the "weaker
sex." She starts right off with a sign language trying to communicate with the nationals who are taking care of her luggage. Right away, the missionary
who is meeting her may groan and mark her off as
"another independent old maid on our hands!"

It is not easy to suddenly drop the self-sufficient
role, bow to authority, and start being a lady, especially if you happen to be able to manage things

quite well — perhaps even better than the man in the crowd. Some girls can. But if you want to fit into your missionary task as a woman the way God intended, a woman you will have to be. If you don't want to be tagged with the obnoxious title of "independent old maid missionary," you will have to work at it and ask the Lord daily for wisdom, help, and balance.

Balance is one of the most difficult things. For while you must be under authority and must be ladylike, you must also be independent to a certain extent, and more self-sufficient than the wives on the compound.

What about the odd jobs around the house that a husband does? There are some jobs that a girl cannot do, or should not have to do, if there is a man anywhere around. That is particularly true of heavy lifting and major mechanical and carpentry jobs. But a girl can learn, if she doesn't already know, how to fix the plug of an iron or a lamp, how to adjust her sewing machine, how to paint a cupboard, and a multitude of other household tasks. You don't have to be masculine to know how to do a few things. Being feminine doesn't mean you are helpless and have to make a nuisance of yourself.

When you ask someone's husband to do a job for you, be aware that probably his wife is impatiently waiting for him to take care of a dozen odd jobs in his own house. Don't take up his time by asking him to do trivial things that you, with just a little effort and thought, could have done yourself. You not only make a pest of yourself but also may put a dent in your friendship with his wife.

You will discover that if you don't cry "wolf, wolf" every time you need a little odd job done, then when you are really stuck and really need assistance, both the husband and the wife will be delighted to help. They will admire your pluck at tackling the minor jobs and will be ready to give you a hand with the major ones.

In the missionary work which puts you beside a man, you can be a lady without making demands on him. He doesn't want to treat you as a fellow man because you are not.

Show him the common courtesies that make him feel manly. Don't forget that it is as important that he feel and act like a man as it is for you to be a lady. Don't pick up a heavy typewriter and lug it across the room in front of him — even if you do have the muscle. If you approach a door at the same time, step back and let him open it for you if it is convenient for you to do so. Naturally I am speaking of the fellow worker who comes from a background where the code of ethics and etiquette is the same as yours.

Give him every opportunity you can to be manly, and he will respect you for it. If a fellow missionary gives you a gentle rebuke for not allowing him to be a gentleman when he could have been, take it with a grin of thanks, and don't forget next time. Remember, nearly everyone wants you to be what you want to be — a lady. It is pretty easy to forget sometimes on the back side of some missionary deserts.

I recall one lesson I learned the hard way, but learned well. When I returned from a furlough, it was necessary for me to live with a missionary couple for a few weeks. My trunks and cases were stacked in a corner waiting until I could get an apartment of my own. One day I needed something from one of my trunks and went after it myself. I didn't want to bother the busy man of the house.

In moving things around, I had to lift a very heavy footlocker. I managed to move it all right, but the handle broke. When the metal corner landed on my big toe the pain made me crumple on the cement. For several minutes I was too paralyzed to move. By the time my host returned, I was in the living room, soaking a badly swollen and very black toe. Despite the words of sympathy, he was furious with me and in no uncertain terms told me it served me right for not asking for help. I learned my lesson well. You can be sure that I never moved one of those trunks again.

Be careful with your personal grooming habits. Just because there are no eligible bachelors around, this is no excuse to become sloppy. Take a long look at yourself every now and then, and decide whether or not you have let your personal appearance slide because of lack of outward incentive. Be the well-groomed "you" that went on deputation before going to the field.

Some of you are, or will be, sweating it out in the roughest of jungle or bush in a primitive environment. Others will be in smart-dressing city areas. Cultures differ, and attitudes of the nationals have to be taken into consideration. You won't want to offend the national Christians in the poorer areas by dressing too elaborately. The opposite may apply in the more advanced areas of the world. It is not the clothes themselves that are important. They must fit your working surroundings at your own discretion. What is most important is your attitude toward your own personal appearance.

Your hair is important. It makes a tremendous difference in your appearance. Keep it clean and attractive, even though you may style it simply. If you are working in a part of the world where humidity and heat take the curl out, try to adopt a style which will be becoming even if it is straight.

Your personal appearance is important for your morale, and, believe it or not, for the morale of your fellow workers. And who knows, someday you may suddenly encounter an available, desirable bachelor. Don't hold your breath, but be ready!

Unfortunately, many missionaries have all the outward qualifications of a lady, but fall short in the basic spiritual issue of being the womanly women God wants them to be. Why do so many of us balk at submitting to masculine authority?

Often girls have to do important jobs, even pioneer work, because there is no man to do them. But what happens when a man becomes available for the job? The girl feels slighted and hurt because she may be asked to hand over her responsibility to a man.

Take, for example, a very responsible girl I knew. Her responsibility on her mission station was the financial department. She kept the books, which involved paying the rents and making numerous financial transactions with the local nationals. She did a good job and was highly commended by the mission leaders.

As the work grew and expanded, a full-time financial manager was needed for the job, someone who had more bookkeeping experience and training than she had. In time he arrived on the scene — a capable young married fellow of twenty-five.

The girl whose job he took over almost fell apart. Her world of responsibility collapsed around her, and life was pretty miserable for her and all those with whom she worked. I remember once she complained almost hysterically to me that if that young upstart who didn't know anything about anything took over everything would certainly go to ruin.

It was very apparent that she considered him a personal affront. Although she didn't realize it, her biggest problem was that she was not willing to turn over her authority to him, even though the weight of the responsibility was far too much, physically and mentally, for her to carry.

When a woman wants to keep or gain authority when there are capable men around, it usually spells trouble. (There may be God-ordained exceptions, but they are few and far between.) The whole thing often festers into an unpleasant sore of self-importance. And if anything will brand her a difficult old maid, that will. On the other hand, there is nothing that will sweeten and refresh one's own femininity more than to quietly say "yes" to the Lord and to the authority over her. Everyone will think more of her for it.

Another situation may involve a girl without her

even realizing what is happening. Most mission executives have secretaries — good ones. The problem comes when he must be away from his office. It is very easy for the secretary to assume command in his absence, even though some other man may actually have the position of authority while he is gone. Secretaries have been known really to make men miserable in such cases. It can also cause resentment among the wives and other single girls.

Some girls arrive on the field with chips on their shoulders against men. It may be the result of a single unpleasant experience or result from the fact that the men in her background — father, brothers, or other relatives — have not given her cause to respect men. The girl covers her hurt and distrust by proving herself sufficient and efficient without men. This automatically makes her resent the authority of men, and the attitude is carried over into her missionary work.

I knew a girl who had been hurt very badly. Although she knew that her attitude toward men and manhood was wrong, she could not seem to give the hurt to the Lord sufficiently to allow his sweetness to fill the bitter vacancy the hurt had left.

She was one of the most attractive girls I have ever known. The more simply and modestly she dressed, the more attractive she was. The men were usually electrified by her.

She had a brilliant mind along with her good looks, and the field director never had a better secretary. Her work was flawless. He would gladly have given her a greal deal of responsibility, enough to challenge a mind that was very difficult to challenge. But her attitude toward men stood in the way. It showed itself in an air of superiority which she demonstrated around them and was marked by a very sharp tongue. Intellectually she *was* above most of them, and she did not hesitate to make them feel it, often leaving them humiliated and speechless.

She lasted on the field just one year. No, she wasn't sent home. She felt that the secretarial work was not challenge and fulfillment enough for her intellect. Little did she realize that patience and sweetness, qualities of a true woman, would have rewarded her with all the challenge that she needed.

I have never been more sick at heart than when she left. We were close friends. But neither she nor the people with whom she worked could have been happy as long as she remained in that condition. Only after she left, when several of the men expressed their feelings, was the basic problem impressed on me. For a woman to work successfully with men there is the absolute necessity of a God-given respect for manhood and the willingness to accept a man's authority when the situation demands.

God puts a high premium on true womanhood, too. To win the title of a feminine, godly woman from your fellow missionaries, you will have to measure up to God's definition of a true woman. It's what he intended you to be. Peter says, "Be beautiful inside, in your hearts, with the lasting charm of a gentle and quiet spirit which is so precious to God" (1 Peter 3:4 TLB). Take time to read the thirty-first chapter of Proverbs for yourself. The qualifications of a godly woman are laid on the line there. And how many women of God are mentioned by Paul in his writing.

Most of the women in the Bible are spoken of in connection with their husbands, but that does not change the picture for the single girl. God's pattern of behavior for a woman is the same — married or single. To follow it is to make yourself not only what he wants you to be, but also what others will praise you for being.

Ask God to fill you with the fragrant spirit of true womanhood as he meant it to be. Then lavish it on those around you, those to whom he has called you to minister, and those with whom he has called you to work. You will find satisfaction and fulfillment in your life and the result will certainly be blessing.

7

"... AS I HAVE LOVED YOU"

Elaine sat listlessly in the chaise longue in the middle of her room. She stared through the window across the dusty mission compound. She was momentarily oblivious to the heat of the tropical day that made her clothes cling to her like flypaper.

She had been walking back to her house after teaching the women's Bible class a few minutes ago. As she stepped around the corner of the house, Sarah and Naomi, ahead of her on the path, had glanced at each other, then at her, and then had hurried off in separate directions. But not before Elaine overheard them say, "... loves God so much, why doesn't she love Pastor Tom?

Conflicting thoughts invaded her mind. She suppressed a little feeling of guilt as she thought, "So I'm not crazy about Tom. But surely it doesn't show that much."

A tide of resentment rose in her as she thought of her fellow missionary. They ought to know Tom as she knew him. Then they wouldn't be so quick to criticize her for her lack of love. Oh, there wasn't anything so terribly wrong with him. He did his work. She had to admit, too, that he was sincere enough. And he was thoroughly loyal to the mission and to the Lord. But somehow he always managed to rub her the wrong way without even trying. Sometimes she even suspected he did try.

Maybe it was the way he made such a big deal out of every little thing. It was particularly bad now that the regular field director was on furlough, and he had been filling in as Mr. Swanson's substitute. There had to be conferences about every little matter that came up. She was sure that if Tom's cat had kittens he would call a compound conference to decide what to name them. And everything was always so hush-hush. He might tell everybody the same thing, but he acted as if he were sharing a secret with each one. His sense of importance really ran away with him.

He irritated Elaine to the core. It was only with concentrated effort that she kept from blowing her stack at him. It was crazy, she supposed, to let it bother her so much. She had come to the place where she could hardly bear him, and she had to admit to herself that she had sounded off a few times. Unfortunately, she remembered now, Sarah had been there on one of those occasions.

As Elaine's thoughts tumbled on, the Holy Spirit

began gently, but firmly, to do his work. Projected suddenly into her mind was the verse "By this shall all men know that ye are my disciples, that ye love one another." The truth of that verse which she knew so well now seemed to stun her. Was it possible that Sarah and Naomi might doubt her love to the Lord because they knew she had no real love for Tom? Could her witness to them actually be ineffective because of her attitude toward Tom? Surely they would reconsider when they thought about how much she loved them. And she really did love them. She longed to see them come to know the Lord — her Lord.

And she had done a lot for them, particularly for Sarah. She had sat with her day and night when her little boy had been so ill. And how many times she had given her clothes and food. She had talked to Sarah so many times about the Lord and what he could do for her. The girl had listened attentively, but there was always a slight reserve.

". . . loves God so much, why doesn't she love Pastor Tom?" As the words continued to burn, Elaine reached for her Bible. "By this shall all men know . . ." Let's see. Where was it? Should be in the thirteenth chapter of John. Yes, there it was, near the end of the chapter. She read it slowly to herself as if she had never seen it before. "By this all men will know that you are my disciples, if you have love for one another" (RSV).

Thoughtfully she scanned the next page. There was a lot more on the subject. "This is my commandment, that you love one another as I have loved you. Greater love has no man than this, that

a man lay down his life for his friends. You are
my friends if you do what I command you" (John
14:12-14 RSV).

That really gave her a jolt. She was commanded
to love Tom as much as Christ loved her? But that
wasn't possible. Surely the Lord could not really
have meant that. How could you possibly love a
person who irritated you to the core? How could
you possibly love a person as much as Christ did?
After all he is God!

Perhaps one of her more recent Bible transla-
tions would make it more clear. She reached for
her copy of *The Living Bible,* and there it was
again. "I *demand* that you love each other as much
as I love you!" "Demand"! That one word
leaped from the page. Painfully Elaine looked away
from the open Bible. For a long time she sat there,
her eyes swimming with the tears that at last spilled
over. A confused feeling of helplessness, frustration, and repentance churned in her heart. She
knew she had miserably failed her Lord.

Desperation tinged her broken spirit. "Lord, I
have failed you and my fellow missionaries, and
Sarah and Naomi, and others so terribly. O Heavenly Father, forgive me. What can I do? You know
I have no love of my own for Tom. It just isn't
there. But Lord — Lord, I'm willing to love him if
you will only fill my heart with your love and give
me a right spirit toward him."

". . . and put a right spirit within me." That was
the cry of David's heart. It is the cry, too, of every
Christian who is sincerely and desperately seeking
to please the Lord with a right spirit and right atti-

tudes, attitudes governed by the Holy Spirit.

How easy it is to replace right attitudes with wrong ones. They slip in so softly, so unnoticed. The flesh and the devil see to that. Then you become aware of them but don't want to face them for what they are. You try to hide them, suppress them, cover them over with a good coat of varnish so that at least others won't know how you really feel. Sometimes the cover-up job can be pretty good, too. At least it looks good from the pulpit or while you're talking to an outsider.

But things begin to leak at the seams. You will discover that it is impossible to work day by day with fellow missionaries and completely cover your lack of love, the jealous heart, the discontent, irritation, anger, or a tendency to seek self-glory. Then to your shame you realize that those you have been seeking to win for Christ have been closely watching your life to see if what you preach really does make all the difference you say it makes. And they have not been fooled.

Constantly allowing the love of the Lord to control your motives and attitudes is the basic ingredient of all right attitudes. "Love for the brethren" is the clearest sign of a victorious Christian life. Somehow it can not be faked by the flesh, no matter how hard you may try. Are there certain people — Christians, even — you just can't seem to love? Your personalities clash head-on. There are too many things on which you can't see eye to eye. The harder you try to love them, the more your efforts seem to betray your real feelings. If it depended on your show of human love for the breth-

ren, would people know that you are a disciple of
the Lord Jesus?

But we are *commanded* to love one another. It
must be possible, even if you are humanly incapa-
ble of it. God never asks anything of you which he
is not able to fulfill in you if you allow him to do
so. That, of course, is the heart of the matter. Love
for every fellow Christian is found in Christ, and
only in Christ. You must reach out and trust him
for it. There is love there, with plenty to spare:
love that will even make it possible to love a fellow
missionary who, at least in your thinking, is totally
unlovable. Remember, "I demand that you love
each other as much as I love you!"

A lack of love is not the only out-of-place attitude that may plague a missionary. Grumbling is
another. Mission authorities usually bear the brunt
— and sometimes the bruises — of that one.

A favorite line of the grumbler is, "Nobody ever
tells me anything!" She (it could be *he*) seems to
think that because she does not know all the inner
workings of the mission leadership or because she
is not given a complete account of all the discussions and deliberations in the field director's office,
she is being deliberately left out. She may feel especially slighted if she has not heard the latest
"problems" of the other missionaries.

To begin with, there are usually reasons why
mission authorities do not reveal everything. One
obvious reason is that they do not have the time to
tell all the details to everyone or to mention every
item in memos to the staff. If there is a new type
of work or ministry in the planning stages, it would

only be confusing if nebulous and uncertain ideas were circulated among the general staff. And, of course, the mission leadership never makes a habit of publicizing the faults and problems of fellow missionaries. That certainly does not help to correct or improve wrong attitudes.

There are some missionaries who constantly grumble about the lack of money. Could the lack of money be caused by their inability to spend what they have wisely or with a disciplined sense of stewardship? First Corinthians 7:17 says, "As God hath distributed to every man, as the Lord hath called every one, so let him walk."

Another Scripture particularly applicable to grumblers is this: "Do all things without grumbling or questioning, that you may be blameless and innocent, children of God without blemish in the midst of a crooked and perverse generation, among whom you shine as lights in the world . . . (Philippians 2:14, 15 RSV).

A dangerous outgrowth of the habit of grumbling is the gripe session. It would be shocking, I'm sure, to know the number of missionaries who have had to go home because they started airing their grievances and dissatisfactions to other workers. What starts as simply airing a few dissatisfactions can grow into sessions of criticism — all, of course, behind the back of the mission administrators. The gripers stir each other up so much that every little fault of the "other side" is greatly magnified. Insubordination quickly develops. The situation suddenly becomes impossible, and they pull up stakes to demonstrate some great principle, or they be-

come such a hindrance that the mission has to send
them home for the good of the work. And the
devil sits back and laughs while more souls go to
hell. The annals of mission organizations are
shamefully stained with the accounts of groups, families, and single missionaries that have left the field
for that very reason.

Run fast from anything that even hints at the
spirit of dissension. You may be inclined to agree
with the gripes. You may even have a few legiti-
mate ones of your own to add. But trying to solve
the problems by grumbling or by packing up and
leaving is not the solution. Remember, the Lord
called you to this very place under the authority of
this mission.

If there really is a problem, first pray about it.
Then if there is still a problem, you can legitimately
take it to a mission leader or someone in authority.
Take it to the top if you have to, but don't talk behind people's backs. If you feel you cannot talk to
mission authorities about the situation, or if your
answer is no, then pray some more, and more —
and more. Be honest with God. You may be the
one who is wrong, you know. Ask God to change
you, the circumstances, or the mission's feelings in
the matter. Perhaps all three need to be changed!
Don't just mention it to God in passing. If it is a
situation that makes you desperate, then it is a situation about which you should be desperate with
your Heavenly Father.

The act of taking your problems and complaints
to your fellow workers implies that you do not
really believe that your Heavenly Father is able to

solve the problems. Sometimes you say by your actions, "I don't want the Lord to solve the problem. I want to do it myself."

It is not always wrong to take problems to a fellow missionary, but do so only after you have honestly and fervently prayed about it. Some of the things you fuss about may not be your own problems at all and are really none of your business. Certainly the fires of dissension are only fed by criticizing instead of praying. Can you gripe and still say, "The Lord has first place in my life as a missionary"?

Next on the list is the persecution complex. This is one attitude that is particularly devastating. Missionaries who are afflicted with it feel that everybody is always against them and what they are trying to do for the Lord. If they weren't spending so much time trying to enhance their own reputations, they would not be so upset. Where the Lord has first place, there is little opportunity for the start of a persecution complex.

And then there are the "glory hounds." They show up in every occupation, and missions are not exempt. There are a couple of types. Some are constantly talking about how much they are accomplishing. They are always giving personal reports of the great results to the mission leadership — and anyone else who will listen. There are others who put in an enormous amount of overtime, even at the expense of their bodies and their health. Their goal is to build a good reputation or to make someone feel sorry for them. While they are usually impatient with the work and shortcomings of others, their own work shows little real result. Again, where the Lord has first place, there is little opportunity for being a "glory hound."

Missionaries can also be jealous — jealous of another's opportunities, talents, or abilities, or worst of all, jealous of a fellow missionary's spiritual fruitfulness. Jealousy can bring about deeper, more serious suffering to more people than almost any other wrong attitude. Guard against it with all the grace the Lord can give you.

What Christian has not heard of Hudson Taylor? Do you realize that the effects of Hudson Taylor's early efforts were nearly destroyed by a new missionary who, after three months on the field, decided he would not lower his dignity to eat with chopsticks and dress like a Chinese. Jealousy of Taylor's authority was at the root of the problem. The result was incredible suffering. For a time the mission was split down the middle. Only when the Lord brought them all back to their senses through the tragic death of one of the Taylor children, was the rift closed. Even then, two couples and a young girl were lost to the mission. Can jealousy start where Christ has first place?

Another attitude which can completely ruin both the personal life and ministry of a missionary is bitterness. Single girls seem particularly vulnerable. Bitterness is often the product of self-pity. Or if you have been wronged in some way, bitterness can settle over you like a heavy cloud of gloom. Even failure to see converts in the work or to be appreciated by the nationals can cause real bitterness.

What is the answer? Ask your Heavenly Father to set a daily watch over your heart attitudes. You may do your work well; but if you are not laboring in the love of the Lord, your missionary life will be in vain. If there is fruit from your labors, you must recognize that it was not because of you, but in spite of you. Labor without love will bring little reward.

"If I speak in the tongues of men and of angels, but have not love, I am a noisy gong or a clanging cymbal. And if I have prophetic powers, and understand all mysteries and all knowledge, and if I have all faith, so as to remove mountains, but have not love, I am nothing. If I give away all I have, and if I deliver my body to be burned, but have not love, I gain nothing.

"Love is patient and kind; love is not jealous or boastful; it is not arrogant or rude. Love does not insist on its own way; it is not irritable or resentful; it does not rejoice at wrong, but rejoices in the right. Love bears all things, believes all things, hopes all things, endures all things" (1 Corinthians 13:1-7 RSV).

8

SUITABLE SUITORS

"Suitors — on the field I'm headed for? From what I've heard, there hasn't been an eligible male on that barren stretch of landscape for many a long year!"

Don't be too sure!

There may be two or three types of suitors who toss roses across your path. The roses may smell sweet, but some have devastating thorns if you try to grasp them. Some aren't even safe to smell or look at too closely.

It's understandable that "falling in love" with the available man is the peculiar temptation of the single lady missionary. How does a girl keep a proper perspective on men, when the days stretch into years without any really satisfying masculine companionship?

Do the nationals begin to look like good prospects for romance despite your dissimilar cultural background and way of life? Does it begin to seem that it must be the Lord's will for you to marry one of them? Believe it or not, it happens often. Statistics reveal that a surprising number of girls decide to marry into the culture to which they came to minister. Unfortunately, it appears that the results are usually disastrous, causing heartbreak and an end to the ministry to which God called them.

Why is it so easy to get into this problem situation? There are many reasons. One, of course, is that a girl may get to know certain nationals very well through working closely with them. Discussions are apt to bring you even closer because heart issues are the very reason for being on the field.

Differences in color and culture by no means prevent physical attraction. Every nation has handsome men! And every culture has men who are intelligent, witty, and winsome. When you see these men day in and day out, become friends and even co-workers, it is very natural that they begin to look more and more like eligible prospects for marriage.

Couple these factors with deepening loneliness and longing for masculine fellowship, and you have a situation made to order.

Some girls fall prey to the suggestion that they can better minister to the people if they marry into their culture. I recall hearing three or four single girls discussing that possibility one day. They were talking about marrying into a culture where the

women were not even considered to have a soul
and were, of course, treated accordingly by their
men folk. How could a missionary possibly think
it would aid her ministry? Foreign women were
respected for their own culture, which gave them
enough prestige so that they could teach and minister. If they had married into the national culture,
by that very act they would have been silenced.

One missionary friend of mine married into the
culture to which she was ministering with the
thought of furthering her ministry. After a great
deal of heartache, they ended up back in the United
States, where they have been ever since — in secular work.

One mission has lost a number of its girls to national marriages. Again, most of the marriages
have turned out to be unhappy. One reason is that
in that particular culture the husbands beat their
wives about once a week. It is supposed to show
they still love them enough to be jealous of them.
You can imagine how well that goes over with a
woman of North American background! Oh yes,
it's easy to smile from a distance, but how would
you react if you were in the same situation?

Another couple were of the same color, but different national cultures. She came to minister and
before long married a local pastor. They have continued to have a fruitful ministry because of her
sweet submission, but she has suffered deeply in her
personal life.

Some girls, yielding to loneliness and temptation, ignore the social mores of the national cul-

ture. Loss of respect and damage to the ministry often results. One girl I know stood and talked to one of the Christian workmen on the compound in the twilight of early evening. They were in plain sight of everyone. After a second such incident, one of the national pastors became so upset he threatened to disassociate himself from the mission for fear his reputation would be harmed by the scandalous proceedings on the compound.

I had a discussion one day with that same pastor, a very godly man, about the widely variant social customs of our cultures. I mentioned that I had been alone with a fellow in a car until as late as eleven or twelve o'clock, that we had had good social and spiritual fellowship together, and that he had never even presumed to touch me. That pastor looked at me and shook his head. "If I did not know you well," he told me, "and your life before the Lord, I would say you were lying. Even in my thinking, as a Christian pastor, that is impossible."

It was a forceful lesson to me in the necessity for understanding the culture to which I had come to minister and a frightening revelation of how careful I must be in my manners and Christian walk before them.

Some girls blindly tell themselves that their special friend must be different than the other men in his culture. He is so sweet, so romantic, so tender. Be honest with yourself, with the Lord, and with him. Take a good long look at the wives in his culture. Is that how you think you'll be happy? Don't fool yourself. Life won't be any different for you than it is for them, no matter how romantic it may seem at the moment. Their marriage relationship may not cause them unhappiness; but, by its very contrast with your way of thinking, you will find it very difficult, if not impossible, to be happy in the same circumstances.

How, then, does one avoid this pitfall? It all goes back to that matter of day by day commitment. Day by day cast yourself on God. Don't entertain "it could be possible" thoughts and dreams. Anything looks possible and right to the infatuated lonely heart. Remember that the enemy of our souls is very good at laying traps. If it will knock you out of commission — the Lord's commission — Satan will mine every inch of your pathway and toss a few grenades at you too. Don't be embarrassed to literally flee temptation if you have to. The Lord understands our need to flee at times, or he wouldn't have told us to do so. Don't worry about saving face. The Lord will see to that. He'll save all the face you need.

A less thorny rose may come your way, but even *it* needs to be clasped very lightly. A bachelor passing by may stop in your town, or even your bit of bush country. He may be a college student visiting different mission fields. He may just be a Christian tourist who is interested in local missionary work. Or he may have a specific ministry elsewhere and have stopped by on business. Perhaps he's a friend of one of the other missionaries.

Enjoy his casual friendship and friendliness as far as circumstances permit. You need masculine fellowship. The Lord may even have allowed him to come your way to fill that definite need or to help you remember what the Christian men of your own culture are like. He may know that you just need to feel like a woman again.

But guard your heart! Your first consideration is your place of ministry. Don't forget it. Furthermore, even if you rush this type, they seldom fall. Their thoughts are elsewhere, and often their hearts are too. Don't start thinking immediately, like some girls I know, "I wonder, now, could the Lord have sent him here just to meet me?" Then they start letting their imaginations run wild trying to juggle the pieces of their two lives together so they will fit. You know: "We both like to fish, we both majored in psychology, and we both like dogs. We could even sing together!" You found that out in the first conversation you had with him. Rarely do those circumstances produce a God-ordained romance, even though you may know of a case where it actually happened. Romantic imagination is a fast horse that will become a runaway in minutes if it is given the least bit of encouragement. And runaways nearly always produce some minor wounds, if not something worse. When he is gone, disappointment burns deeper than your former boredom.

In this general class of bachelor passersby, there may be a real Don Juan, the one who rushes *you,* giving you a flatteringly good time, raising false hopes. He leaves behind not merely a disappointed heart, but a broken one. And while you are on your knees before the Lord asking him to mend the broken pieces, the bachelor is on his merry way, feeling he's done a lot to give a poor single missionary girl a real lift.

Have you ever heard the saying, "Love which is only an episode in the life of a man is the entire history of a woman's life"? Ask the Lord constantly to give you a wise, discerning heart.

One other bouquet of roses may come your way, but don't hold your breath until it comes. Occasionally an honest-to-goodness single man may join the mission and even get as far as your field without attachments. He may be a "confirmed bachelor" who never will get married, but then again he may not be. He may be the one the Lord has sent just for you. After all, oceans do not limit the working out of God's perfect will. I have at least five personal friends who have married under those circumstances.

However, you'll do well to diligently, even desperately, seek God's will in the matter. Don't trust your own wisdom. You are too close to the circumstances. Even if it seems right, your backgrounds and personalities may be so different that only unhappiness would follow marriage. Unfortunately that has happened too. Sometimes a strong, independent-minded woman will marry a weak-willed man who is unable to handle her. It bothers me a great deal to see this kind of marriage relationship. It cannot be a very good testimony to the nationals, nor can it be a very happy marriage. Sometimes, too, girls who have enjoyed their independent, self-sufficient lives, may after the romantic wedding is over, rebel at having to submit themselves to a husband. They don't really want the responsibilities of a family and home, which of course involves curtailing, to some extent at least, their own personal ministries.

Renew your commitment again and again with "Lord, I want your will at any cost." Then if that bachelor is still there — yours from the Lord — ring the bells! And may the Lord bless you both!

By the way, if real, God-given romance *does* come your way, don't be frustrated by the surveillance of the mission or of your fellow workers. You can expect them to be curious and interested, just as your family would be if they were around. They *are* your family in the Lord. It is quite natural for them to sit back and watch. They love you and are interested. More than that, they are thrilled for you if they see the Lord's hand in it all. Don't resent their teasing or the feeling of being in a fish bowl. You know the old saying, "If you can't fight it, join it." Go along with their teasing, and take it for what it is: a sign of the warmth of affectionate hearts who are genuinely interested in your happiness.

"Joining it" does not mean that you have to tell everyone about your private affairs, especially when things aren't sure yet. You don't need to be quick to ask everyone's advice. In fact, you'll probably be happier if you don't. If you really need counsel, talk to one person whose confidence you can trust and whose advice you can count on.

Even with all the surveillance and interest of your fellow missionaries, you can still keep the fun and freshness of personal romance. You can even have the fun of making others just a bit curious, if you keep your mouth shut. Let them guess a little. Let them wonder. But don't resent the curiosity. Turn it to happy, joyful fun; and you'll have a wonderful romance, not only enjoyed by yourselves, but by everybody else too.

9

CREATIVE FELLOWSHIP

Coconuts don't make very good bowling balls. You can't roller skate on the jungle floor. The nearest golf course is five thousand miles away. Oh, for a place to go skiing or boating! It is even fifty miles to "dinner out"! There is no concert to attend, not even a youth singspiration or a YFC rally on Saturday night.

Not all missionaries are stripped of all the activities they used to enjoy for entertainment or relaxation or refreshment. But a good share of them have to face this difficulty and you may be one of them. What do you do to satisfy the side of you that craves fun? Deprived of all the familiar places and activities, are you tempted to look at the ceiling in your relaxation time and feel sorry for yourself?

Only when the handy North American entertainment crutches, both secular and religious, are swept from under your feet will you discover just how dependent, or non-dependent, on them you have become.

You are fortunate if you have been brought up on the farm or in the backwood or some other situation where you've learned to provide your own fun for entertainment, where there's no one but you and perhaps a handful of others to be the source of fun. But if you've lived in a whirlpool of social activity all your life, as many girls have, then you have an adjustment ahead of you which will take conscious effort and a great deal of the Lord's help.

Increasingly missionaries are living in two decidedly different types of environment. Mission work is still done in the primitive areas, where the ministering is still done from village to village, from hut to hut. But there are also large concentrations of missionaries in big cities now. Emphasis on the student ministry, missionary radio stations, Bible school work, literature work, and hospital ministry has brought this about. There are also cities where several missions have established their administrative offices and from which they supervise their outreach. This means that the social needs of the missionary and the possibilities for socializing will differ a great deal from place to place.

The girl in the jungle definitely has the rougher time and must make more of a concentrated effort not to become defeated by loneliness and homesickness. Here there is also greater danger for her to become too emotionally involved with one or two other workers. That is the reason why many missions no longer place one single girl on a station with one married couple. The odds are too great that there will be unhealthy relationships, especially if the girl has real social needs.

Remember this above all: the God who called you to the field is able to supply all your needs according to his riches in Christ Jesus. He did not call you in order to dump you in a defeated heap of loneliness in the jungle. The key to victory in this is the same as for every other problem. It is in your personal relationship to Christ. He is your friend and companion, as well as Savior and God. Treat him that way.

There are also practical things to do to keep from being eaten up with loneliness. If you have very few people with whom to socialize, then the record player, the tape recorder, the table games, the jigsaw puzzles, the books, and the hobby material you brought with you in those barrels will become very important. Anything creative you can do will substitute for company and bring a real measure of personal human satisfaction.

You will, of course, socialize with the others on the station. If you have kept your relationship with your fellow missionaries fresh and guarded it against familiarity, then the occasional social times you can have with them will be wonderful times of fun and fellowship. Playing games, banqueting in real style, showing pictures, or even working on joint hobby projects can all be enjoyed together. Much, of course, depends on the personalities involved.

In socializing with a limited group of faces and personalities, unselfishness must be a real part of the fun. People often have strong likes and dislikes about certain forms of entertainment. Bluntly stating a dislike can put a real damper on any fellowship that might be enjoyed around it. It could sound like this: "I can't bear to work on jigsaw puzzles. It seems so childish to spend time putting a picture together and just tear it apart again!" Or, "Monopoly? Jim gets too hot under the collar dealing for property." Or perhaps, "I don't like to play Scrabble. I never win, and besides Sally always takes too long to make up her mind."

Perhaps you would do well to take a close look at the purpose of entertainment in your life. Is it a means to an end? It most certainly should *not* be. If it is, you're on the wrong track. The purpose of any relaxation activity should be to relieve the mind and relax the emotions and spirit from the tension-building problems of the work in which you are involved. It should be a time that will refresh your hearts and spirits to be better able to accomplish the work God called you to.

If you play games "for blood," you may as well forget them. They'll only bring more tension to you and everybody else. Be sportsman enough to try to win, but be a gracious loser. If you aren't, ask the Lord to make you one. He can, you know, if you really want him to.

Make a conscious effort to enjoy what the other person enjoys, even if it is very difficult at first. If you go into it wholeheartedly, prejudices forgotten, you just may begin to appreciate the activity yourself. Why not take the attitude that what gives another joy, gives you joy as well. If you are unselfish, that won't take too much effort.

There are other things, of course, which are involved in playing some kinds of games. Some people have a real conviction that using any type of playing cards in a game is wrong, while you may have no such personal conviction about it; or the situation may be in reverse. Always respect the other person's convictions and never belittle him. I have known people who were addicted to gambling when they were unsaved, and to them any card game savors of the life from which they were set free. It genuinely offends them to see Christians playing games that make use of cards.

There may also be opportunity for some social life with the nationals, depending on where you are and your particular situation. Often there are national workers with whom you can have wonderful fun and fellowship and your social contacts can be a blessing to their lives.

Don't overdo anything — even innocent games can spell bondage. Your interest in them will soon wear thin and become just another factor in your boredom. Or if you become addicted to a game, it can rob you of the time you should be spending with the Lord or spending in your ministry. (Oh yes, it really does happen to missionaries.) Also, over-socializing with the same small group can produce tensions which will cause more fatigue than relaxation!

Every person is a social being — some more, some less so. You must guard against using forms

of entertainment to fill an empty, restless spirit
that should be filled with the joy of the Lord. *That*
comes from a close walk with him and necessitates
spending time with him.

The missionary girl who lives and works in the
large city, surrounded by associates and many visi-
tors traveling through, obviously has her social life
made. In many places there are even outside
sources of entertainment. There are also many
good restaurants for that special night out. In fact,
you may have more opportunity for social activities with real friends than you ever had at home.

If that is the case, your problem will not be how
to drum up entertainment, but how to keep social
activities in proper perspective to your work and
ministry. It is easy to let them become an end in
themselves. If you are not careful, your "soul-
catching fishing boat" on which you occasionally
have some times of pleasurable relaxation will become a "pleasure craft" on which you sometimes,
in your spare time, do some gospel work.

It may sound like unlikely that this could happen to a missionary girl, but it does happen more
often than you think. I have seen missionary girls
load themselves with so many social activities that
their spiritual lives, and hence the work which they
came to do, has suffered. One girl confessed that
it was hard to keep her mind on the Wednesday
evening prayer meeting for thinking about what
they were going to do after it was over.

Socializing and over-socializing can make tired
bodies and cause leanness of soul. I know. I have
been caught in the trap a few times. I finally came

to the place where, with the Lord's help, I said to myself and occasionally to some very insistent friends, that anything that hindered my early-morning hour with the Lord from being what it should be just had to go. It simply was not worth it. That has cut out quite a bit at times, because if I am to be at my best for my mission responsibilities, I just have to have eight hours of sleep.

Some missionary girls use social times to invite unsaved acquaintances. It is a very good idea if you can use the time as a real avenue of testimony. But one must give a word of warning to girls who would ask unsaved bachelors to their social times. If you are not alert to the implications, you may become dangerously involved. What happens when you begin to be really fond of that non-Christian friend? What happens if he is attracted to *you?* What do you do when he decides to bypass the social gatherings and ask you out to dinner "to repay you for all your kindness" or just "to get better acquainted"?

Do you start praying extra hard for his salvation — and ask others to do so too, and at the same time launch an intimate friendship? Apart from the Lord's grace, it is bound to end up in heartache, frustration, or total chaos in your life. You say, "But my situation is different. I can't say no to him. It may drive him away from the Lord." Is it you or the spirit of grace that will draw him to the Lord? Without realizing it, you may cause him to become harder to the gospel by a compromising friendship. Don't forget that the world often sets higher standards for the Christian than we do ourselves. That unsaved friend is far more apt to sit up and take notice of you and your gospel if you say a gracious no and tell him the reason why. Satan can fit a temptation to you and your exact situation so that you will see every reason why you should make an exception to God's principles of behavior for a Christian. He is especially good at setting up traps involving romantic social situations. He knows just how vulnerable single missionary girls are in that spot.

What about your annual vacation time? Where you spend it and with whom will depend largely on your own mission's arrangements and your location. In many areas of the world, particularly in the more primitive areas, missions have set up their own vacation resorts where the climate is healthful and relaxing. In other parts of the world, especially the more populated parts, you can probably choose where you want to go and what you want to do. It will then depend largely on your financial resources. Most missionaries can't often afford to take elaborate vacations.

Whatever your ideas are about vacation time, remember why the mission has given you a vacation time. It is in order that you may have some time away from your work, to be renewed in body, soul, and spirit. That means that your vacation should be mostly rest — real rest and relaxation. Try to avoid spending any great amount of your vacation time traveling. At least try not to do that on every vacation. It is nice to see places and sights you have never seen before, but if it leaves you more tired than you were to begin with, you've completely defeated the purpose of your vacation time. It is not fair to the mission, the Lord, or yourself to start another year all worn out.

You do well to seek as much guidance from the Lord concerning your social times and your vacation time as for any other part of your personal life. In the total picture it is just as important to glorify the Lord in this area of your life as in any other. Your social life will always bear a direct relationship to your ministry.

10

DISCIPLINED RELATIONSHIPS

Close contact with the other missionaries on your station is inevitable. That means there will be close relationships with the families as well as with the single girl with whom you will probably live. Of course there are exceptions. Girls do at times work alone on a station, but more often there are missionary couples near who will be your constant associates.

In your relationship to the families there is great potential for happy fellowship, the sharing of laughter as well as tears, both hard work and relaxation, spiritual victories and defeats. But in that relationship and association lies also the raw material for unpleasant incidents which may send missionaries home and stain the cause of Christ with shame.

It's not a subject we like to discuss. But turning

our backs and pretending the problem is not there does not eliminate it. It is important to know what causes the tragic stories familiar to many, if not most, mission headquarters. What are the things that stack up to make jealous wives, unhappy families, sour husbands, and bitter single girls?

No one knows all the answers, but I believe there are a number of things the single girl can do, or avoid, to prevent ugly situations from arising. She *can* be a real blessing to the family and help to avert dangerous problems.

The most important relationship you, the single girl, have to maintain is with the wife. Write in mural-sized letters on the wall of your mind, "What makes the wife happy makes me happy." Value her friendship, because an open and complete understanding of each other will be the most direct path to a happy relationship with the whole family.

Take time to get to know her. Don't expect her to seek you out. Her home responsibilities very often won't permit that. Find times when you can be alone with her; don't pay social calls only when her husband is home. It is important that she know you well and know you as a friend. With the confidence of your friendship, her mind will be at ease when she thinks of you and her husband working together.

If you know the wife well, you will understand what things bother her and be aware of little things you should be careful about in your relationship with her husband. You will thus have a far greater sense of freedom, understanding, and an absence of strain, in your contacts with her husband.

Get close to the wife, but never become overly familiar with her. It is very unwise for a wife to pour out her marriage problems to a single girl, especially a close associate. If she tries to, steer her away from it quickly, and help her to seek her solution from the Lord. If she really needs to have someone's advice, suggest another couple. It may be very tempting to you to try and solve her problems. The answer may be very obvious to you. It is very flattering to a "wish-I-were-married" single gal to be asked advice by a married person, but it is far from wise to find yourself in the middle of their personal problems. By being there, you may very well add to the problem.

You say, "But if she asks me, doesn't that mean she has confidence in me?" Not necessarily. We women are funny creatures, you know. She may trust you completely, but when you start giving her the advice she asks for, she may begin to question why you seem to understand her husband so well — perhaps even better than she does. At that point jealousy may be added to the problems she already has. Refusal to discuss their marriage is the best policy.

When you've done all you can to ensure a good relationship and understanding with the wife, she still may be jealous. Ask yourself *this*: "If I were his wife, would I be jealous too?" If you can put yourself in her place, you may gain some insight. An amazing number of small things can stack up to make a tied-down wife jealous.

Living alone, yet liking to cook, I often unloaded

my goodies on my working companions. They happened, in this case, all to be husbands. I soon found out that it wasn't a smart idea to present chocolate cake to a married co-worker too often, especially when it was his favorite, and more especially when his wife was not able to make it often or, as it happened, quite as well. On thinking about it, I really couldn't blame her. Could you?

Don't worry too much about a husband's stomach if his wife doesn't happen to be the world's greatest cook. Don't feel sorry for him. He married her because he loved her. He has other compensations. Food is far from being the most important thing in life. He needs to learn that if he hasn't done so already.

Speaking of food — you may find yourself in the middle of another embarrassing experience. Men can be very thoughtless at times. (That, of course, is not to say that thoughtlessness is limited to their half of the human race.) You may wish you could use a paddle where it would do the most good when, after your guests have finished eating, the husband turns to the wife and says, "Why can't you cook like that?" Even though he may smile and be teasing, believe me that hurts any wife, especially if she knows she *can't* "cook like that"! What do you do? Hold your breath and say something that will help the wife out, even if you have to stammer something stupid like "You're terrible! Patty ought to give you bread and water for the rest of your life!" Then change the subject — fast.

If things get a little tight and busy, or even hectic because of illness at their house, don't be too quick to jump in and help. Ask the wife if you can help her. But if there's even a hint that she'd rather let the housework go than have outside help, particularly from a self-sufficient single girl, back out gracefully. You may be defeating your own sincere, good purpose if you insist on helping her out. Sometimes the last straw for a tired, discouraged wife is to have another girl bounce into her house and give her the feeling she is a failure at housekeeping.

If the wife is in the hospital or has to go elsewhere without the family, don't go to their house and help out the husband, even if he is really stuck. If it is essential that you help with the children, take them to your house. Don't entertain children and husband. If he is a rather helpless husband, he can with a little effort learn to be more self-sufficient. This may be common sense, but there are some girls who seem never to have heard of common sense. I have known girls who wouldn't hesitate to steam in and take over, thoughtlessly feeling they were performing a wonderful act of kindness.

Be considerate of a woman's time alone with her husband. It will probably be precious little, and they don't need a social call from you every other evening. If she asks you over — fine. Otherwise, make yourself scarce when they are home together.

Be casual, but careful, about accounting to her for any unusual amount of work time spent with her husband. You don't have to be in bondage about it; however, just a casual word will be reassuring.

It would be impossible to put down on paper all the little ways in which you can assure the wife of the propriety of your relationship with her husband. There are hundreds of little ways in which you can help her to be happy in spite of the close ties it is necessary for you to have with her family. Ask the Lord constantly to help you to be sensitive to her needs and to show you how you can help her. As far as your relationship to her and her husband is concerned, make yourself responsible to the Lord for her happiness.

Don't just go halfway — go all the way. Maybe you don't owe her an explanation about something, but give it anyway. Maybe an incident wasn't your fault. Explain it with regret anyway. If she shows jealousy and then feels bad about it, talk to her about it. Show her that you don't blame her for her feelings. Keep short accounts with her. If you know she is questioning something, talk to her about it. You may never know the complicated reasons — physical, emotional, and spiritual — that have made her feel jealous at that moment.

It is equally important to safeguard your relationship to the husband, especially if you work with him as well as live on the same mission compound. You are fortunate if the husband with whom you have to deal is as aware of the need for carefulness in his relationship to you as you are. However, that is not always the case. In fact, it happens frequently that men are quite thoughtless along these lines. They may not intend any harm, but

sometimes they ignore the implications of a particular situation. And it naturally follows that the
more thoughtless the husband, the more jealous a
wife he has at home.

Although there is a wide difference in human
makeup, it is the woman's responsibility and priv-
ilege to uphold standards of behavior. Rarely will a
man, especially a Christian man, resent or step
over the lines that a girl sets down. He will have a
higher regard for her, even if he has been sternly
rebuked.

Without being a prudish legalist, it is important
to have a clear-cut set of guidelines in your mind.
If you think things through now, you may save
yourself and the husband from unintentionally getting into some very awkward situations.

One of the most carefully-drawn lines in your
mind should be concerning discussions of a personal
nature — spiritual or otherwise — when you are
working alone together. Your personal affairs are
none of his business, nor are his your business.
This is a common pitfall. If you work together constantly, it is a very big temptation.

It is altogether possible for a man to begin to
feel you understand him better than his wife does.
And you may feel the same way. Perhaps you do
understand him better. Possibly her care of house
and children has at least temporarily taken up the
time she should spend with him, the time when
she should be an understanding wife. Perhaps they
never have understood each other well, but that's
not your problem. Your understanding heart will
certainly bring him no closer to his wife. His per-

sonal life is simply none of your business. He is married — and not to you. Whatever his problems, they are between himself, his wife, and the Lord. Your understanding counsel can only magnify the problem.

"But," you say, "he insists on talking to me about his personal affairs. I can't be rude." Why can't you? If it will prevent a broken home and another missionary tragedy, you certainly must. You can be nice but firm at the same time. Unless he is not what he should be, he will respect you for it.

I recall one husband who thought he was a specialist in analyzing others' personal complexes. (He had plenty of his own to talk about as well.) Several subtle attempts to slide him off the subject failed. It finally took a flat: "I've never made a habit of discussing my own personal affairs or those of my co-workers. I'd rather not start now." That was that. He may have been a bit embarrassed, but I've had no problem with him since, and there has certainly been no loss of respect or good will.

To keep a close guard on discussing *your* affairs with him is even more important. He is a man; you are a woman. It is even more awkward and embarrassing for him to have to rebuke you for familiarity. Because of the woman's responsibility to hold the line, it makes it much more difficult and embarrassing for both of you if he has to.

It is a great temptation for a girl to pour out her troubles to a man, just because he is a man. It happens often. What can the man do? He can offer you advice, which he really isn't in a position to do. Or he can tell you to come over and talk to him and his wife when they are together. That will make your face red. Face it honestly. Often it is not just because you know his spiritual advice is so wonderful, it is because he is a man. If the husband does not have what it takes to stop the heart-to-heart talk sessions which you initiate, then you are headed for trouble.

I often hear a girl say, "He is just like a brother (or a father) to me." He is neither. He is a man — no relation — and men are men all the way to ninety and beyond.

Avoid asking the husband to do things that would make an awkward situation for him. Because he is a gentleman he doesn't like to refuse to help a woman. Neither does he want to put his wife in a bad light by insinuating that she wouldn't like it. By all means do not ask him to do things that would bring you together at night. If it is necessary to have his help at that time, graciously ask the wife to come too for a cup of coffee. Nothing — not anything — is worth risking the Lord's name, everyone's happiness, and your own reputation as well as that of your co-worker.

Please do not forget that we have an adversary, the devil. 1 Peter 5:8 in the Phillips translation begins, "Be self-controlled and vigilant. . . ." This is especially appropriate when coupled with the remainder of the verse from *The Living Bible*: ". . . Watch out for attacks from Satan, your great enemy. He prowls around like a hungry, roaring lion, looking for some victim to tear apart." You aren't facing just human circumstances over which you may have complete control. Besides the natural human temptations of the flesh, you are facing a spiritual enemy who will stop at nothing to get you out of his territory which you have invaded.

Just a word about your relationship to the children in the families on your station. Here is a chance for a very wonderful friendship, but don't allow your motherly heart to become possessive of them. It is easy to steal affections that belong to busy parents, causing great heartache.

I recall one missionary family with an adorable little four-year-old — their only child. He spent most of his time begging to go up the road (if he wasn't already there) to be with "Aunt Sally." It is very easy for a single girl to become attached to a child and to steal his affections. Sometimes the single girl has more time to spend with the children than their own parents.

The reverse situation may also arise. The parents may try to get you to take care of their children every chance they can. You never need to feel obligated to baby-sit for a family. Their children are the responsibility God has given them. Make it clear to them in a nice or even humorous way. If you always give in to them, you certainly won't be aiding their sense of responsibility to their children. Of course, there are times when you will be happy to baby-sit for them. It would be very nice of you even to offer now and then so that they can have a free evening alone together. That is, of course, if there is some place to go or a restaurant at which to eat on special occasions.

Every problem situation in this chapter is taken

from real life. The experience of every missionary, single and married, is beset with pitfalls of temptation in the everyday affairs of life. We do well to face them frankly and honestly. Daily heed must be given to the admonition of the Apostle Paul: "Put on the Lord Jesus Christ, and make no provision for the flesh, to gratify its desires" (Romans 13:14 RSV).

11

SELECTED FOR SATISFACTION

Lazily Elaine stretched out on the deckchair. It was sheer luxury to her tired body. As she gazed at the scattered white puff clouds backed by blue, blue sky, a tinge of excitement rippled through her. Home at last! She was actually going home on furlough. She used to joke that it was her ambition to be a missionary home on furlough. Now that the time was actually here she was both excited and scared. It was frightening to think of facing people as a "real live" missionary. Would they expect too much of her?

She could have flown home. The mission had given her the choice. But, as anxious as she was to get home and see her family, she had chosen the boat trip. She felt she needed it to collect herself. She needed to have time, away from all responsibility, to spend with the Lord — before jumping into the fast-moving stream at home.

Elaine fingered the journal-diary on her lap. In it were recorded a whole term of thoughts and feelings and happenings. Most of it she had written during her daily quiet times. It was filled with accounts of struggles, victories, defeats, joys, and sorrows.

Her quiet time had become the most essential part of the day to her. At first she had often allowed other things to crowd out that time alone with the Lord. Surely her service for the Lord was just as important. But she soon learned that without close daily communion alone with the Lord she became easy prey for all sorts of temptation. A devotional time was even a help physically. It was altogether a practical fact that the "joy of the Lord" was her strength.

Elaine liked to think of her heart as her own private sanctuary, a sort of chapel. She could commune there with the Lord any minute of the day or night. But there were also the daily times of purposeful worship and intercession for the needs of others, a definite time set aside to spend with him.

The Lord had become more real to her during this term of service. It was in part because she had learned to take everything to the sanctuary, even for a fleeting moment when she felt particular need of his guidance. Sometimes it was a quick opening of her heart to receive the special provision of the Lord's love for someone. What a relief it had been for her to discover that the Lord did not condemn her for her lack of love. It was only sin when she failed to allow the Lord's love to be sufficient where her love so miserably failed.

At times she just took a minute to run in and tell the Lord that she loved him. Those times were always sweet and refreshing. She wondered if David hadn't had something like this in mind when he wrote: "One thing have I asked of the Lord; that will I seek after; that I may dwell in the house of the Lord all the days of my life, to behold the beauty of the Lord and to enquire in his temple."

At times she had failed to take things to the sanctuary and lay them before the Lord. Instead she had done things her own way. The inevitable result was spiritual defeat and frustration. Sometimes it had seemed she would never learn to let the Lord of her sanctuary control certain situations.

She opened the journal and began thumbing through its well-worn pages. The ink on some pages was smeared by tears. Some entries brought smiles, others a blush of shame. Some brought tears to her eyes as she recalled a victory gained after long defeat.

She couldn't help but be amused at her first entry. She had written it the day she had arrived at the port city.

> April 2: I was just stepping off the gangplank when near panic seized me. I seemed to be hemmed in by oppressive tropical heat. Chattering porters squeezed up to me, their bare backs and chests glistening with smelly sweat. Obnoxious smells — oppressive heat

> — strange people. It made me dizzy. I struggled to reach the waving hands and smiling faces of the Swansons, the missionaries who were there to meet me. Suddenly I was seized with an overwhelming sensation. These strange, smelly people were the ones I had come to tell about Jesus! I am here — on the mission field! The place I have dreamed about, prayed about, and planned about for so long.

It rambled on with her first impressions, but Elaine skipped to a later date. She sighed as she looked at the entry for a week later. It was the first (but by no means the last) negative mention of JoAnne.

> April 10: It seems I'll never get settled, and JoAnne is no help. I can hardly move, it seems, without her telling me where I should put something or how I should arrange it. To hear her talk and give advice, you'd think she'd been here for ten years. She got here just a few weeks ahead of me. O Lord, do I have to have roommate problems?

As Elaine stared out over the endless succession of waves pushing their way to the horizon, she thought of her long struggle over JoAnne. She blushed just thinking about the day she had begged Mr. Swanson to "do something" about it. That day, though, had marked the beginning of a real change in the situation in their apartment. With her desperate heart she had gone to the sanctuary that day. Only then had she realized that she had been battling much of the time over JoAnne in her own strength. She was just struggling to settle the whole thing in her own way. She was trying to make it go the way she wanted it to go. It was then, when she began to lay it all out before the Lord in her quiet time, that she began to realize just how vital that time with the Lord was every day.

Slowly at first, the relationship with JoAnne began to improve. She found more patience, more love. She was sure it wasn't her own. The Lord had given it to her. Outward circumstances had not changed a bit, but she began really enjoying JoAnne. Instead of resenting her commanding ways so much, she just ignored them. What real difference did it make if JoAnne tried to boss her around? She didn't have to do what she said. Sometimes she would just grin at JoAnne when she got started, and that seemed to get through to her more than anything else. Strange. She knew it could only be the Lord who had taken away the resentment. She used to get so mad when JoAnne was officious.

Other problems had been solved in the sanctuary. Some of them were so sticky that she hadn't been able to tell another soul. They were problems that involved personal temptation. Strength to resist had been found only in a daily cry to the Lord in her early morning time with him. The Lord had taken her through one day at a time.

She had discovered something else. Often during her first years on the field, she had gotten terribly upset about the problems of other missionaries.

She and JoAnne had many long sessions about
these apparently insoluble problems of others. She
had realized later, when she was really honest with
herself, that she had sort of liked just raking the
whole thing over with JoAnne. It made her feel
more "in" somehow, especially when they ex-
changed bits of information that the other one
didn't know about. But strangely enough, their
discussions always left her more upset than ever.
She was sure it had left JoAnne with the same feelings. It had been very hard to face up to that one.

One day as she was reading in *The Living Bible,*
Ephesians 6:12 hit her head-on. "For we are not
fighting against people made of flesh and blood, but
against persons without bodies — the evil rulers of
the unseen world, those mighty satanic beings and
great evil princes of darkness who rule this world;
and against huge numbers of wicked spirits in the
spirit world."

It was the first part that got her. ". . . Not
fighting against people . . ." Wasn't she? Weren't
they? Every time she turned around there seemed
to be a feud of some kind between some of the
missionaries. She was very much a part of it. The
Holy Spirit would not let her escape on that one.

How the enemy had hoodwinked her! He kept
fellow missionaries fighting each other. She should
have been on her knees battling the satanic forces
of darkness. How much time she had wasted! She
had not recognized the source of many of the problems among them. She had kicked against the
problems and the personalities involved. How often she had denounced the weaknesses of fellow

missionaries. She had failed to see that the "wicked spirits in the unseen world" constantly fought against them. They maneuvered their weaknesses in the flesh if they could not strike them head-on. Elaine realized that by not praying for her fellow missionaries, by not claiming victory over the powers of darkness for them, she had actually been a party to their defeat.

A broken prayer for forgiveness was recorded for that morning. She had also written in black and white, as a self-reminder, her determination to pray fervently, instead of talk.

Bit by bit she had discovered that problems which had seemed impossible to solve could actually be prayed through to the solution. It shouldn't have been so amazing to her. After all, she had heard all her life that "God answers prayer," but seeing for herself was something else.

Some problems were solved; others just seemed to evaporate. A few real problems among the workers still remained, but now it only seemed a greater challenge to pray. What an exciting adventure, to watch God work in the open as she prayed in private!

Sometimes she told herself, "Elaine, the fact that you've been praying doesn't mean that is why the problem is solved." But she was always rebuked in the spirit for that thought. To say that the answer had not been the result of request (of course she realized that often others were praying too) would be to deny the very promises of God. Wasn't it James who had written, "The effectual fervent prayer of a righteous man availeth much." Righteous?

Her? That used to stick, too. But graciously the Lord had shown her that the righteousness of Christ was hers.

Solved problems weren't the only blessings her time in the sanctuary had brought. Elaine had learned that the throne was the source of very practical supplies. How many times the Lord had supplied her financial needs in answer to prayer. There was, for example, the money for the car. From a human standpoint it was impossible to raise money for a car out in the bush. But the Lord had raised it for her. She had scarcely begun to pray until from here and there, all unexpected sources, the money for the car had begun to come in. She had mentioned the need and asked people to pray about it in a prayer letter home, but the Lord had motivated people to give.

There had been other victories won on her knees. As she prayed for the salvation of those to whom she ministered, the Lord began to work. The angels in heaven weren't the only ones who rejoiced the day Sarah and Naomi had finally put their trust in the Lord. She had wept for joy — joy that they had come to know the Lord and that the Lord had overruled her own inconsistent testimony in front of them. She had confessed to the Lord and to them her lack of real love for Tom. She had wondered at the time if it would not set them back spiritually. On the contrary, the Lord in his grace had used the incident to bring them even closer to accepting the Lord. And finally they did. But it had not been before she had stormed the gates of heaven.

Her quiet time in the sanctuary had not just been a tool of ministry — an asking place. It was the place where she had gotten acquainted with her Heavenly Father. His love to her became so very real. He was not only God; he was her Friend, her Companion. She had learned the meaning of Psalm 96:6, "Strength and beauty are in the sanctuary . . ."

She was more aware every day of the great need to walk closer. And sometimes she saw herself only on the threshhold, looking in on all that God had for her. Her heart at times seemed to burst with the feeling of expectation.

Through it all he had brought a deep sense of satisfaction in himself alone. Oh, sure, she would still like to marry if the Lord brought someone — the *right* one — along. In fact, she felt more prepared for marriage than she ever had before. But now she knew that marriage wasn't necessary to find completeness and perfect human fulfillment and satisfaction. She had experienced all of that in Christ.

Her thoughts were interrupted by the musical gong as the dining steward made his way around the decks. She hadn't read very far in her journal. But as she stretched and began to walk, a bit stiffly, toward her stateroom, it seemed that the ocean sunshine had flooded her heart.

P.S.

Don't ask for a picture of Elaine. She is not one person, but a composite of many real girls. The problems, the struggles, the temptations — they are all genuine. Illustrations have had to be kept deliberately anonymous, but they are no less true. Most important is that Elaine's *victories* are real too. So is her discovery that all she longed for personally is found in Christ.

Best of all is that what she has experienced in her service for Christ is there for *you* too.

Do you want it?